WHEN KINGS KNEEL

⸻ ❧❦ ⸻

THE STRENGTH OF A SURRENDERED MAN

SHOLA ADEGOKE

WHEN KINGS KNEEL
The Strength of a Surrendered Man

Copyright © 2025 Shola Adegoke

Paperback ISBN: 978-1-965593-58-5

Published by Cornerstone Publishing

A Division of Cornerstone Creativity Group LLC

Info@thecornerstonepublishers.com

www.thecornerstonepublishers.com

Author's Contact

To book the author to speak at your next event or to order bulk copies of this book, please, use the information below:

http://www.sholaadegoke.com/

Info@sholaadegoke.com

Printed in the United States of America.

DEDICATION

To the men who chose the altar over applause.

To the fathers, brothers, sons, and mentors who taught us that kneeling is not weakness; rather, it's where true strength begins.

To every man fighting silent battles, rising after failure, and leading from a place of humility and healing - this book is for you.

And most of all,

To the King of Kings, the Almighty God, the One before whom every crown is laid down, every heart is made whole, and every king finds his true identity.

This offering is Yours.

FOREWORD

The author of this book, Shola Adegoke, served under my leadership as the minister in charge of the youth ministry. During that time, he exemplified the very characteristics described in this book: he was friendly, supportive, and uplifting. His impact has remained unmatched since then.

This book encourages men not to give up, acknowledging that human nature has been affected by sin and that its consequences are felt everywhere. It also highlights that men's unique responsibilities expose them to spiritual attacks, inner struggles, and socio-cultural challenges.

The author urges men not to succumb to despair, fear, or shame when they feel vulnerable. Instead, he advocates for seeking help from God and utilizing all available human resources when faced with pain.

To reinforce his points, the author draws wisdom from scripture and contrasts it with stories of men who have risen from adversity to achieve greatness.

He effectively uses the limited space in this book to address key issues, concluding each point with positivity, declarations, and relevant prayers.

Those who must conquer and reign must learn to kneel.

Thus, the author calls all men into consistent prayer. endeavoring to win God's favor through their character.

"The men who change the world aren't the ones with perfect résumés. They're the ones who've wrestled with God, knelt, and got back up, transformed"

Pastor Dele Salewon
Senior Pastor – RCCG New Covenant Parish
Oklahoma City, OK

CONTENTS

ACKNOWLEDGEMENTS

To my beloved wife, "Fisayo"—thank you for being the calm in my storm, the strength behind my surrender, and the quiet voice that constantly reminds me I am more than enough in God's hands. Your love, wisdom, and unwavering faith have shaped not only this book, but the man I continue to become.

To my precious children, may this book be part of the legacy I leave for you. I pray it helps you see that strength is not just in standing tall, but in kneeling low before God with courage, humility, and conviction.

To my Mom and my Parents-in-law, thank you for your legacy of honor, discipline, and faith. Your sacrifices continue to echo in my life, and I pray this work brings joy to the foundation you laid. Especially, to my late Dad – I hope I've made you proud.

To my dearest brothers, sisters, brothers-in-law and sisters-in-law, thank you for the constant encouragement, fierce love that covered me through seasons of stretching. You inspire me in more ways than you know.

To my pastors, "Pastor Ayo & Layide Ajayi and entire Salvation Center Katy — thank you for standing as watchmen on the wall, your leadership, and leading with truth, love, and unwavering conviction. You represent one of God's finest.

To my mentors and spiritual parents, Pastor Dele & Moji Salewon - thank you for your spiritual covering and the way you model surrendered strength. Your examples have helped shape the heartbeat of this message.

To Pastor Gbenga Showunmi and Cornerstone Publishing - thank you for birthing this vision. Your dedication and professionalism is top-notch.

To Bishop Francis-Wale Oke and Rev Victoria-Tokunbo Oke - true spiritual trailblazers Your legacy of surrendered leadership and prophetic fire has shaped this work and continuously inspires a generation to bow before the King of kings.

And finally, to every man who has ever felt the weight of the crown and the call to kneel—this book is for you.

All glory belongs to God, the King of Kings

HOW TO USE THIS BOOK

When Kings Kneel is not just something to read; it's something to live. Each chapter weaves together stories, Scripture, and prayer points designed to speak to the heart and move you toward lasting change. The more intentionally you engage with it, the deeper its impact will be.

Here are three ways you can walk through it:

1. Read Alone - A Personal Journey

Set aside 15-20 minutes for each chapter. Begin with a short prayer, asking God to open your heart. Read slowly, giving space for the words and Scriptures to sink in. When you reach the prayer points, don't just read them - pray them out loud or write them in your own words. Keep a journal nearby to capture any convictions, insights, or action steps.

2. Run a Group -A Brotherhood Journey

Gather a few trusted men: friends, family, or brothers from your church. Agree on a pace, perhaps a chapter per week. Meet to discuss the main insights, share how they apply to your lives, and pray through the prayer points together. The honesty, accountability, and encouragement of a brotherhood can turn these chapters into shared victories.

3. Take a 30-Day Challenge - A Focused Journey

Commit to reading one chapter a day for 30 days. Begin each day with the main Scripture and reflect on its meaning, then read the chapter. Choose one clear action to apply that same day. End by praying through the points provided. This concentrated approach can build spiritual momentum and accelerate transformation.

No matter which path you choose, don't rush. Let the words work on you, challenge, and reshape you. This isn't just about finishing a book; it's about becoming the kind of man who leads with strength, walks in humility, and follows Christ without reservation.

INTRODUCTION

This book is not about behavior modification. It's about a holy reorientation.

It's not another "how to be a better man" manual. You've had enough of those.

This is a call; a disruption, a mirror, and an invitation.

Somewhere deep inside, you know there's more than what you've settled for. Beneath the pressure to perform, to provide, protect, and to never show weakness, there's a quiet ache to be whole again, to walk in strength without the mask, to lead with purpose without losing your soul, and to fight for what matters without pretending you're okay.

But you cannot step into that kind of manhood standing tall. You have to kneel.

The world teaches men to rise; be louder, tougher, and more visible. Strength is often measured by dominance, status, or how much we can carry without complaint. But in the Kingdom of God, strength isn't defined by how high a man climbs; it's defined by how low he's willing to kneel.

You were not created to carry your calling alone. You were not designed to build legacy while limping in silence. And no man, no matter how gifted, respected, or broken, can find life while hiding behind performance.

The men who change the world are not the ones with perfect résumés. They're the ones who've wrestled with God, surrendered their pride, and refused to bow to culture's cheap version of manhood.

They're the ones who knelt and got back up, transformed.

This book was born from a fire; a burden for men who carry silent battles, buried pain, unseen potential, and a sacred call that often gets drowned in noise. Whether you are a husband, father, leader, builder, or brother trying to keep it together, this book is a letter to your soul.

It is a collection of letters - heartbeats on paper. Each one written to sons, brothers, husbands, and leaders - men like you. We'll talk about heavy things: identity, purity, failure, emotional pain, calling, sexual struggles, vision, finances, and legacy, not from a pedestal but from the floor.

Each chapter is a letter, a prayer, a reminder, and a call to action.

Some of these letters will feel like quiet conversations. Others might shake you a little. They are all written with love, truth, and deep respect for who you are and who you're becoming.

I don't claim to have all the answers. But I do know this:

There is a throne above every kingdom, a name above every title, and a King who longs to meet you - not when you have it all together, but right here, where you kneel.

Let's begin the journey, not by rising, but by kneeling, because when kings kneel, everything changes; families heal, legacies shift, and whole nations can be changed.

CHAPTER 1

REMEMBER WHO YOU ARE

A Letter to Men about Their Identity in Christ

Dear Brother,

In a world that constantly tries to define us by our failures, salaries, relationships, or our past, it's easy to forget who we truly are. But God never forgets.

Let me tell you a story about the **"restoration of Josh."**

Josh was a contractor who had built homes for others, but couldn't seem to rebuild his own life. After a failed marriage, a broken business partnership, and years estranged from his son, he felt like a ghost walking among men. He started telling himself, *"I'm just a disappointment and damaged goods."*

One day, he wandered into a small church in work boots and dust-covered jeans. He didn't mean to stay, but something about the quiet worship pulled him in. At the end of the service, the pastor read this verse: *"Therefore if any man be in Christ, he is a new creature: old things are passed away; behold, all things are become new."* - 2 Corinthians 5:17 (KJV)

That verse struck him like lightning. The pastor went on, "You are not your failure, not your past, and not what left you or what betrayed you. If you are in Christ, you are a new creation."

Something broke in Josh. Not shame, but chains. That day, he didn't just hear the truth; he *believed it.* And that belief began to rebuild the man. Today, Josh is not perfect, but he is rooted. He now serves and has reconciled with his son. When he tells other men about grace, his voice carries the weight of someone who knows what it means to be restored.

Brother, it's time to awaken to the truth of who you are – **"The Real You."**

Your identity is not based on performance but on **position**. If you are in Christ, then:

- You are **accepted** in the Beloved (Ephesians 1:6)

- You are **chosen** by God (1 Peter 2:9)

- You are **forgiven** of all your sins (Colossians 2:13)

- You are **an heir with Christ** (Romans 8:17)

- You are **not condemned** (Romans 8:1)

- You are **God's workmanship** (Ephesians 2:10)

You are more than a husband, father, worker, or leader. You are a *son of the living God*, and that never expires, even when everything else does.

So, remember to stand tall again.

The world doesn't need more men who chase status; it needs men who remember who they are. Maybe that's you today, standing at the edge of your breakthrough, dusty from life's battles but beloved by the Father. Before you say *"I'm too far gone"* or *"I'm too broken"*, remember this: God doesn't build on the perfect; He builds on the *available*.

Come home to who you already are in Christ.

As you reflect on these words, find a quiet, comfortable space and lift these prayers from your heart. Know that you are not alone; many men across the world are kneeling with you to discover their identity.

PRAYER POINTS - IDENTITY IN CHRIST

1. Lord, I thank You for making me a new creation. Your Word says, "If any man be in Christ, he is a new creature; old things are passed away; behold, all things are become new" (2 Corinthians 5:17). My past is gone. And by Your grace, I now walk boldly in my new identity.

2. I am not a slave but a son, for "we are all the children of God by faith in Christ Jesus" (Galatians 3:26). Remind me daily of who I am in You.

3. Thank You for the authority You've placed on me. "As many as received Him, to them He gave power to become the sons of God" (John 1:12). I receive this power with joy and responsibility.

4. Let my life reflect Christ in every thought, word, and action. "I am crucified with Christ: nevertheless I live; yet not I, but Christ liveth in me" (Galatians 2:20).

5. May I never lose sight of my royal calling. You have made me part of a chosen generation, a royal priesthood, a holy nation, set apart to show forth Your praise (1 Peter 2:9).

6. Keep my heart anchored in Your grace and far from condemnation, for "there is therefore now no condemnation to them which are in Christ Jesus" (Romans 8:1).

7. Let my life shine like light in a dark world. "Ye are the light of the world. A city that is set on a hill cannot be hid" (Matthew 5:14). Use me to reflect Your glory wherever I go.

8. I choose victory over victimhood, because "in all these things we are more than conquerors through Him that loved us" (Romans 8:37).

9. I praise You, for I am fearfully and wonderfully made (Psalm 139:14). You crafted me with intention, beauty, and purpose.

10. Holy Spirit, bear witness with my spirit daily that I am a child of God. "The Spirit itself beareth witness with our spirit, that we are the children of God" (Romans 8:16). Let my identity be rooted in You and lived out boldly for Your glory.

CHAPTER 2

BE THE MAN WHO STANDS CLEAN

A Letter to Men about Purity and Holiness

Dear Brother,

Purity is not weakness. Holiness is not an impossible standard. In a culture that celebrates indulgence and labels restraint as outdated, God is still calling men to be set apart, not perfect, but pure.

Let me share a relatable story with you about Tolu's **"turning point."**

Tolu was a worship leader in his late 30s, respected, talented, and outwardly solid. But behind closed doors, he battled with pornography and masturbation, which started in his teens, became a "stress relief" in college, and never quite let go. He would repent one week and fall the next. The guilt became unbearable, and eventually, the shame silenced his worship.

One day during a men's retreat, an older gentleman shared how purity isn't simply about behavior but about surrender. He said, *"Holiness doesn't start with shame; it starts with knowing you're loved and worth cleansing."* That hit Tolu deep. That night, he finally confessed, not just to God, but to two close friends, who didn't judge him. They didn't preach but prayed and walked with him into freedom.

Two years later, he leads a small group, specifically for men struggling with addiction. He's not perfect, but he's clean and no longer hides. Most importantly, he knows now that God isn't ashamed to stand with him, even when he stumbles.

Brother, let me refresh your heart on the true meaning of holiness – **"What Holiness Means."**

Holiness doesn't mean you've never fallen; it means you're set apart for something greater than your urges.

"But as he which hath called you is holy, so be ye holy in all manner of conversation; Because it is written, Be ye holy; for I am holy." -1 Peter 1:15–16 (KJV).

"Blessed are the pure in heart: for they shall see God." - Matthew 5:8 (KJV).

Purity isn't just about sexuality; rather, it's a posture of the heart; it's honesty. It is integrity when no one's watching, refusing to exploit others - even mentally, and asking God to clean even the corners you haven't touched in years.

So, get up, Brother, you can begin again.

If you've struggled, you're not alone, and you're not disqualified.

- **Confess it** - Not to broadcast shame, but to welcome healing (James 5:16)

- **Confront it** - Name the triggers. Set the boundaries. Block the exits.

- **Community is key** - You can't conquer darkness alone.

- **Consecrate yourself** - Ask the Holy Spirit to fill the spaces where shame used to live.

God's call is still echoing: *"Be holy."* And His grace still equips: *"I will strengthen thee; yea, I will help thee…"* (Isaiah 41:10)

You are more than your past. You are not what you hide, but who God has set apart. So walk today, not in guilt, but in grace-fueled grit. The world needs clean men, not because they've never stumbled, but because they've chosen to rise again and stand holy.

As you reflect on these words, find a quiet, comfortable space and lift these prayers from your heart. Know that you are not alone; many men across the world are kneeling with you to journey towards purity and holiness.

PRAYER POINTS - PURITY AND HOLINESS

1. Lord, create in me a clean heart and renew a right spirit within me. "Create in me a clean heart, O God; and renew a right spirit within me" (Psalm 51:10).

2. Keep me set apart for Your glory. You have said, "Be ye holy; for I am holy" (1 Peter 1:16). Let holiness mark my thoughts, words, and actions.

3. Let integrity guide my inner world and truth anchor my decisions. "The integrity of the upright shall guide them: but the perverseness of transgressors shall destroy them" (Proverbs 11:3).

4. Strengthen me to flee youthful lusts and pursue righteousness, faith, love, and peace. "Flee also youthful lusts: but follow righteousness, faith, charity, peace..." (2 Timothy 2:22). Empower me to run from sin and run toward You.

5. Place a guard over my thoughts and my eyes. I make a covenant with my eyes, as Your Word declares: "I made a covenant with mine eyes; why then should I think upon a maid?" (Job 31:1).

6. Let my actions reflect purity and character, not just outwardly, but in the secret places of my heart. "Blessed are the pure in heart: for they shall see God" (Matthew 5:8).

7. Empower me to walk in the Spirit daily, that I may not gratify the cravings of the flesh. "Walk in the Spirit, and ye shall not fulfill the lust of the flesh" (Galatians 5:16).

8. Destroy every stronghold of compromise in my life. "Neither give place to the devil" (Ephesians 4:27). Let no room be found for sin or deceit.

9. Wash me clean from every sin that clings to my life, visible or hidden. "Let us cleanse ourselves from all filthiness of the flesh and spirit, perfecting holiness in the fear of God" (2 Corinthians 7:1).

10. Let holiness be my lifestyle, not just a moment. "Follow peace with all men, and holiness, without which no man shall see the Lord" (Hebrews 12:14). Make my life a testimony that Your cleansing power is real, and Your Spirit is enough.

CHAPTER 3

ONE STEP STRONGER

A Letter to Men on Spiritual Growth and Strength

Dear Brother,

We live in a world that praises instant results; faster, stronger, and better. But real spiritual growth doesn't happen overnight. It's forged in quiet decisions, unseen obedience, and daily surrender. It's not about knowing more verses; it's about becoming more like Christ.

"Here is a story about a brother - **James who learned this the long way around with his 5a.m. walks.**"

James was a single father raising two boys and working two jobs. Church was important to him, but his faith felt shallow; his prayers were routine, and his Bible stayed on the nightstand. One day, after a particularly hard week, his car had broken down, the boys were acting out, and he was feeling spiritually numb. He woke up at 5 a.m., wide-eyed. Instead of scrolling through his phone, he slipped on some sneakers and just started walking.

That early walk turned into a conversation with God. He poured out frustration, asked questions, and said things he hadn't said in years. No church lights or worship music - Just him, gravel underfoot, and a Father who was listening.

The next day, he did it again…and again.

Soon, he was waking up *expecting* that space. His early morning walk turned into a sacred rhythm. He started reading a verse before heading out and praying out loud on the sidewalks while the city still sleeps.

Months passed. His temper softened, his boys noticed the peace, and his faith became more than a routine-it became breath.

James didn't become a theologian. He became consistent. And that consistency built spiritual muscle he never thought he had.

Be reminded, dear Brother: grow daily in strength.

You don't need to have it all together; you just need to show up.

> *"But grow in grace, and in the knowledge of our Lord and Saviour Jesus Christ…"* - 2 Peter 3:18 (KJV).

> *"They that wait upon the Lord shall renew their strength..."* - Isaiah 40:31 (KJV).

Spiritual growth isn't about climbing mountains every day. Sometimes, it's just refusing to give up, putting one foot in front of the other toward God.

Some days you'll feel strong. Other days, you'll feel like James did that first morning - just empty. But strength isn't proven in your feelings; it's proven in your *faithfulness*.

So, dear Brother, what will this look like practically?

- **Daily commitment:** Five minutes in the Word is better than none.

- **Honest prayers:** God responds to realness, not rehearsed perfection.

- **Silence and solitude:** Growth often begins where the noise ends.

- **Community:** Iron sharpens iron. Walk with men who walk with God.

So, keep showing up. Keep walking, praying, repenting, and rejoicing. Some days you'll crawl. Some you'll soar. But if you stay rooted, you *will* grow. And one day, your story may be the next "James" for another man who needs to know that God builds strong men quietly.

As you reflect on these words, find a quiet, comfortable space and lift these prayers from your heart. Know that you are not alone; many men across the world are kneeling with you to grow spiritually and receive daily strength.

PRAYER POINTS - SPIRITUAL GROWTH & DAILY STRENGTH

1. Lord, build in me a life of lasting discipline. Train my heart to love righteousness and exercise myself unto godliness (1 Timothy 4:7). Let my pursuit of You be rooted in devotion, not convenience.

2. Feed me with Your Word daily, O God. I choose not to live by bread alone, but by every word that proceeds from Your mouth (Matthew 4:4). Nourish my soul with truth that transforms.

3. Teach me to wait on You and draw strength in stillness. They that wait upon the Lord shall renew their strength; they shall mount up with wings as eagles (Isaiah 40:31). I rise today by Your power.

4. Let my mind be transformed by truth. Renew my thinking, break every false pattern, and help me be transformed by the renewing of my mind, that I may know Your perfect will (Romans 12:2).

5. Stir a holy hunger in me. I thirst for righteousness, for more of You. Blessed are they who hunger and thirst after righteousness, for they shall be filled (Matthew 5:6). Fill me afresh.

6. Sanctify my mouth. Let no corrupt communication proceed from me. Instead, let my words edify and give grace to those who hear (Ephesians 4:29). Let my lips overflow with truth and love.

7. Help me walk in both love and truth. I choose to grow up into Christ in all things by speaking the truth in love (Ephesians 4:15). Let my walk be marked by grace and boldness.

8. Strengthen me for today's assignment. I can do all things through Christ who strengthens me (Philippians 4:13). Whether small or great, I walk in confidence, clothed in divine might.

9. Fill me afresh with the Holy Spirit. Let me not be drunk with the distractions of this world, but be filled with the Spirit (Ephesians 5:18). Overflow in me, Holy Spirit.

10. Lead me not into temptation. Keep me watchful and prayerful, that I may not fall into weakness (Matthew 26:41). Guard my steps and anchor me in Your presence.

CHAPTER 4

THE KIND OF MAN THEY REMEMBER

A Letter to Men on Family, Marriage & Fatherhood

Dear Brother,

You don't have to be a perfect man to be a present one. You don't have to know every answer; you just have to be faithful to ask the right questions and show up.

Sometimes, we think spiritual leadership in the home means having a verse ready for everything. But it often begins with this silent prayer: *"Lord, help me love them like You love me."*

Let me tell you about a man named Charles and **"his quiet legacy."**

Charles was a mechanic in a small rural town. By the world's standards, he was nothing flashy. No college degree or a fancy house. But his marriage lasted 46 years.

He raised four kids. And every Sunday morning, rain or shine, he gathered his family in the living room to pray before church.

He didn't preach to them - he just lived out his faith in the everyday: opening doors for his wife, fixing his kids' bikes after work even when he was exhausted, and kneeling by his bed at night, whispering names in prayer.

One day at his funeral, his grandson stood up and said through tears, *"Grandpa didn't teach me how to be impressive; he taught me how to be steady, how to show up, and how to follow Jesus at home."*

That's the kind of man whose legacy lives generations deep.

Let me remind you of God's call to the family man.

"But if any provide not for his own, and specially for those of his own house, he hath denied the faith…"
- 1 Timothy 5:8 (KJV).

"Husbands, love your wives, even as Christ also loved the church…" - Ephesians 5:25 (KJV).

"The just man walketh in his integrity: his children are blessed after him." - Proverbs 20:7 (KJV)

You're not just a husband or just a father; you're the gatekeeper- the roof, the safe place. Even when you feel like you're failing, they're still watching and learning.

So, dear Brother, what will this look like today?

- **Marriage:** Love her loudly when no one's watching. Forgive faster. Pray for her more than you advise her.

- **Fatherhood:** Be the same man in the living room as you are in the pulpit or office. Say "I'm proud of you" before they prove anything.

- **Legacy:** You don't leave one someday. You're writing it *today*, in how you respond, listen, lead, and love.

You don't need to be rich to be respected. You don't need to be eloquent to leave a mark. You just need to be faithful, even in the ordinary.

As you reflect on these words, find a quiet, comfortable space and lift these prayers from your heart. Know that you are not alone; many men across the world are kneeling with you to uncover the mysteries of family, marriage, and fatherhood.

PRAYER POINTS - FAMILY, MARRIAGE & FATHERHOOD

1. Lord, make me a godly covering over my home. Help me to provide, protect, and lead with honor. For if any provide not for his own, especially for those of his own house, he has denied the faith (1 Timothy 5:8). Let my leadership reflect heaven's order.

2. Let my love for my wife mirror Christ's love -sacrificial, tender, and unwavering. As Christ loved the Church

and gave Himself for it, may I love her deeply and faithfully (Ephesians 5:25).

3. Fill our household with peace and righteousness. Remove every trace of strife, and let Your blessing rest here, for the curse of the Lord is in the house of the wicked, but He blesses the habitation of the just (Proverbs 3:33).

4. Teach me how to train up my children in truth. Let me instruct them not only with words but with lifestyle. I trust Your promise that if I train up a child in the way he should go, when he is old, he will not depart from it (Proverbs 22:6).

5. Guard my home from every scheme of the enemy. Except the Lord builds the house, they labor in vain that build it (Psalm 127:1). Be the builder and the keeper of this household.

6. Let my children walk in truth and grace. May their hearts be anchored in You, for I have no greater joy than to hear that my children walk in truth (3 John 1:4).

7. Give me patience and tenderness as a father. Help me not to provoke my children to wrath but to nurture them in the training and admonition of the Lord (Ephesians 6:4). Make me a model of mercy and guidance.

8. Cover every generational line with blessing. I walk in integrity today so that my children will be blessed after me (Proverbs 20:7). Let righteousness echo down my lineage.

9. Let my marriage reflect divine unity. What You have joined together, let no one and nothing put asunder (Mark 10:9). Make our bond unbreakable in spirit and truth.

10. As for me and my house, we will serve the Lord (Joshua 24:15). May our home echo Your name with joy, reverence, and full devotion, today and always.

CHAPTER 5

LEAD WHERE YOU ARE

A Letter to Men on Leadership, Purpose & Influence

Dear Brother,

Leadership isn't about titles; it's about responsibility. Purpose isn't just about career; it's about calling. Influence isn't about followers; it's about impact.

God didn't design men to drift through life; He calls us to *lead with conviction*, *live with purpose*, and *leave a lasting legacy*.

Here is a story about Jeremiah, **"the Janitor."**

Jeremiah worked the early shift as a custodian in a public high school. He had no formal ministry title, no Instagram platform, and no corner office, but he was consistent. Every morning, he greeted the teachers by name, encouraged the students he saw, and picked up trash others ignored.

One day, a freshman who'd been quietly battling depression came to him after school and said, "I want to live because you care." Jeremiah was stunned. All he'd done was offer a smile and a simple, "I see greatness in you."

Later that week, the school principal called him into the office, not to clean, but to speak. He said, "You have more influence here than anyone on our leadership team."

Jeremiah never called himself a leader, but Heaven did.

Brother, remember, God defines leadership differently.

"He that is greatest among you shall be your servant." - Matthew 23:11 (KJV).

"Let every man abide in the same calling wherein he was called." - 1 Corinthians 7:20 (KJV).

"Ye have not chosen me, but I have chosen you, and ordained you, that ye should go and bring forth fruit..." - John 15:16 (KJV).

You don't need permission to lead. God already positioned you.

- Whether in your home, workplace, or community, your decisions affect those around you.

- You shape culture by how you show up, especially when no one is watching.

- You carry influence every time you choose integrity over ease and obedience over applause.

Always remember that your purpose is not random.

Leadership is not something we grow into later; it's something we steward *now*.

You're leading someone today, even if it's just the future version of yourself. Walk with God, stay faithful in your assignment, and don't underestimate your reach. Jeremiah never preached on a stage, but he changed lives in a hallway.

So will you.

As you reflect on these words, find a quiet, comfortable space and lift these prayers from your heart. Know that you are not alone; many men across the world are kneeling with you to journey towards leadership, purpose and influence.

PRAYER POINTS - LEADERSHIP, PURPOSE & INFLUENCE

1. Father, raise me as a servant-leader in my generation. Help me to lead by serving, knowing that whoever desires to be great must first become a minister to others (Matthew 20:26).

2. Give me wisdom to lead with humility. I will not rely on my understanding, but I ask in faith, knowing that You give wisdom generously to all who ask (James 1:5).

3. Anoint me to lead with excellence and accountability. Let me examine my work, take responsibility for my actions, and rejoice in fulfilling my purpose with integrity (Galatians 6:4).

4. Let my example point others to You, not myself. May my light shine before men, that they may see my good works and glorify my Father in heaven (Matthew 5:16).

5. Remove every trace of ego from my leadership. Help me do nothing out of selfish ambition or vain conceit, but in humility value others above myself (Philippians 2:3).

6. Keep me teachable, no matter my title or age. A wise man hears and increases in learning; make my heart open to correction and growth (Proverbs 1:5).

7. Surround me with mentors and wise counselors. Where there is no counsel, plans fail, but with many advisers, they succeed (Proverbs 15:22). Place such voices in my life.

8. Connect me with leaders who sharpen and stretch me. I choose to walk with the wise, for he who does so becomes wise himself (Proverbs 13:20).

9. Promote me only as I yield to Your principles. I trust that You will make me the head and not the tail, as I obey Your Word and walk in Your ways (Deuteronomy 28:13).

10. Let Your Spirit be the true source of my leadership. Not by might, nor by power, but by Your Spirit will I rise, lead, and fulfill divine purpose (Zechariah 4:6).

CHAPTER 6

BUILT TO LAST

A Letter to Men on Work & Legacy

Dear Brother,

Your work is more than a paycheck. Your purpose is more than survival. And your legacy isn't something you leave behind someday; it's something you live today.

We are not called to success but to significance; to make eternal impact, not just momentary noise.

Let me introduce you to Mr. Felix – **"The Bricklayer Who Built More than Walls"**

Mr. Felix was a bricklayer for over 40 years. Day in, day out, under scorching heat, he laid bricks with a quiet rhythm and whispered prayers. People admired his precision, but few ever asked why he worked with such care.

Only at his funeral did the depth of his purpose unfold.

A former apprentice stood up and said, "He never raised his voice, but he raised ten of us to become men. While we mixed mortar, he taught us how to respect women, manage money, study the Bible, and pray before we start the day."

Another man said, "Because of him, I met Christ at age 17. He never preached at me. He *lived* the sermon."

Mr. Felix didn't hold a title or lead a ministry, but decades later, his fingerprints remain on homes and hearts across his nation.

That's legacy.

So, dear Brother, your work is sacred, and your purpose is now.

> *"Whatsoever thy hand findeth to do, do it with thy might…"* - Ecclesiastes 9:10 (KJV).

> *"The steps of a good man are ordered by the Lord…"* - Psalm 37:23 (KJV).

> *"A good man leaveth an inheritance to his children's children…"* - Proverbs 13:22 (KJV).

Work is not a punishment in God's economy; it's a partnership. Whether you're a teacher, tailor, pastor, plumber, or an entrepreneur, you are called to build more than walls or brands. You're building witness, shaping atmosphere, and leaving echoes. Every conversation… every faithful decision… every time you choose character over compromise, you're laying a legacy.

Here are 3 ways to build what lasts:

- **Work with worship** - Let your daily grind be an offering. God is not only found in church pulpits; He's in construction sites, classrooms, car rides, and emails.

- **Mentor in motion** - Someone is watching how you move. They may never say it, but your consistency is discipling them.

- **Invest beyond income** - Sow into hearts. Teach your children the Word. Be known for generosity, not just grind.

In closing, let me challenge you with these parting thoughts:

Success is impressive. Legacy is eternal.

Wherever you go today, carry your name like oil, not just for fragrance, but for fuel, because the work of your hands, and the posture of your heart, might raise the next world-changer watching in silence.

As you reflect on these words, find a quiet, comfortable space and lift these prayers from your heart. Know that you are not alone; many men across the world are kneeling with you to find our place in work and legacy.

PRAYER POINTS - WORK & LEGACY

1. Father, let me walk worthy of the calling You've placed on my life. May I please You in all things and be fruitful in every good work (Colossians 1:10).

2. Reveal my assignment for this season. Order my steps according to Your will, for the steps of a good man are ordered by the Lord (Psalm 37:23).

3. Help me not grow weary in fulfilling my purpose. Strengthen me to remain steadfast, knowing that in due season I will reap if I do not faint (Galatians 6:9).

4. Teach me to steward and multiply the gifts You've given me. I will not neglect the gift within me, but stir it up for Your glory (1 Timothy 4:14).

5. Let the work of my hands bring glory to You. Establish the work You've given me, and let Your beauty rest upon all I do (Psalm 90:17).

6. Teach me to labor with eternity in view. Whatever my hands find to do, I will do it with all my might, as unto the Lord (Ecclesiastes 9:10).

7. Align my business and daily work with righteousness. Let every weight and balance in my life reflect Your justice and truth (Proverbs 16:11).

8. Let my legacy outlive me in godly impact. Make me a good man who leaves an inheritance of faith and righteousness to my children's children (Proverbs 13:22).

9. Grant me favor in high places without compromise. May diligence open doors, and may I stand before kings and not obscure men (Proverbs 22:29).

10. Root out laziness and stir productivity in me. I reject the sluggard's way and embrace the diligent spirit that yields results (Proverbs 13:4).

CHAPTER 7

NOT ALONE IN THE FIGHT

A Letter to Men on Brotherhood & Community

Dear Brother,

God never designed men to walk alone.

You were never meant to carry the weight of life in silence, tucked behind a firm handshake and a quiet nod. Brotherhood is more than a buzzword; it's survival, strength, and legacy.

Let me share a story of Emeka's **"circle of fire"** that reminds us why community matters now more than ever.

Emeka was known for his strength. A military vet turned entrepreneur who had built his business from scratch and carried his family with quiet grit. But when the pandemic hit, his contracts dried up, his marriage hit turbulence, and the weight he bore in silence nearly broke him.

He stopped answering calls, showing up to church, and even stopped praying. Until one Saturday, five of his brothers from the men's fellowship showed up on his porch - No appointment. No agenda. Just a bag of food, two folding chairs, and a simple, "We're not leaving. You're not fighting this alone."

They sat, listened, and wept with him. Over the following few weeks, they helped Emeka find his feet spiritually, emotionally, financially, and even got his business moving again.

He later said, "I didn't need advice. I needed presence. I didn't need a savior, I already had one. I needed brothers who knew how to *stay.*"

That's brotherhood.

Below are three Bible verses that reveal the truth about **"The Bond of Brotherhood:"**

"Iron sharpeneth iron; so a man sharpeneth the countenance of his friend." - Proverbs 27:17 (KJV).

"Two are better than one... For if they fall, the one will lift up his fellow..." - Ecclesiastes 4:9–10 (KJV).

"Bear ye one another's burdens, and so fulfill the law of Christ." - Galatians 6:2 (KJV).

So, Brother, what will this look like in real life?

- **Check in without waiting for signs -** Sometimes a simple "How's your heart?" breaks a cycle of isolation.

- **Show up without fixing** - Presence heals more than premature advice.

- **Share your story** - Vulnerability opens the door for true connection.

- **Start small** - Pray together, walk together, build something even if it's just trust.

You don't need a men's retreat to find brotherhood; you just need the courage to invite it.

As you reflect on these words, find a quiet, comfortable space and lift these prayers from your heart. Know that you are not alone; many men across the world are kneeling with you to discover the bonds of brotherhood and community.

PRAYER POINTS - BROTHERHOOD & COMMUNITY

1. Father, surround me with brothers who walk in truth and sharpen my soul. Let iron sharpen iron in my friendships and strengthen my spirit daily (Proverbs 27:17).

2. Let our fellowship be a place of honesty, healing, and growth. May we confess our faults one to another and experience Your healing together (James 5:16).

3. Raise godly men in my city and nation - men who walk in righteousness and bring joy to their communities (Proverbs 29:2).

4. Deliver me from isolation and loneliness. Help me walk in covenant brotherhood, where if I fall, another will lift me (Ecclesiastes 4:9-10).

5. Use my testimony to strengthen others. Let the redeemed of the Lord say so, and may my story be a light to my brothers (Psalm 107:2).

6. Teach me how to raise sons in the faith. Let me entrust what I have received to faithful men who will also teach others (2 Timothy 2:2).

7. Remove envy, comparison, and competition from my relationships. Let me not provoke or seek vain glory, but walk in love and humility (Galatians 5:26).

8. Give me a mentor's heart and a learner's spirit. Help me walk with wise men and grow in wisdom each day (Proverbs 13:20).

9. Make me accountable to others and authentic in life. May the wounds of a friend be faithful, and may truth always find space in our circle (Proverbs 27:6).

10. Unify the men of God across generations. Let us dwell together in unity, building each other up for Your glory (Psalm 133:1).

CHAPTER 8

AWAKEN THE WATCHMEN

A Letter to Men on Revival, Intercession & the Nation

Dear Brother,

God is not looking for spectators; He's raising intercessors. He's not waiting on elections, economies, or empires to shift; He's waiting on *men who will pray.*

Revival isn't an event but a cry; a sacred ache for God to move again in the streets, schools, sanctuaries, and souls of a nation. Every time God shakes a land, He first stirs a man to intercede.

Let me tell you the touching story about Gabriel and his **"prayers that shifted the city."**

Gabriel was a night security guard at a university campus. By day, he was nearly invisible to the students rushing to lectures. But each night, after locking the gates, he walked the grounds, praying quietly for every building, every classroom, and every soul.

No one asked him to.

He'd whisper names of professors. Lay hands on dorm rooms. Intercede for lost youth and broken homes. He called it his "midnight assignment."

One day, a campus revival spontaneously broke out during a chapel service. Students began to confess sins, form prayer groups, and cry out for their friends. The chaplain was overwhelmed - not by the numbers, but by the depth.

When they later traced the spiritual shift, they found a quiet thread. It led to Gabriel. His midnight intercession had broken ground no one could see until the rain finally fell.

Let this truth settle in your spirit - intercession is God's strategy for nation building.

You may never sit in parliament. But on your knees, you can shift policies, protect homes, and push back darkness.

"And I sought for a man among them, that should make up the hedge, and stand in the gap..."
- Ezekiel 22:30 (KJV).

"Wilt thou not revive us again: that thy people may rejoice in thee?" - Psalm 85:6 (KJV).

"If my people... shall humble themselves, and pray... then will I hear from heaven, and will heal their land." - 2 Chronicles 7:14 (KJV).

Revival begins when men become altars, not just asking God to move, but becoming the place where He meets the moment.

So, Brother, how can you stand in the gap today?

- **Pray by name** - for your leaders, city, schools, and church.

- **Weep for what's broken** - let apathy be replaced with holy burden.

- **Gather other men** - create pockets of prayer where pride dies and faith rises.

- **Speak life over your land** - your words are seeds. Sow hope, not hate.

ARE YOU READY FOR THE CHALLENGE?

You're not just a citizen of your country; you're a citizen of Heaven, sent as an ambassador (2 Corinthians 5:20). When you walk the streets, speak in boardrooms, or sit at dinner tables, you represent the kingdom of the One who still heals lands and revives nations.

So rise, watchman. The wall is waiting!

As you reflect on these words, find a quiet, comfortable space and lift these prayers from your heart. Know that you are not alone; many men across the world are kneeling with you to receive the fire for revival, intercession and nation building.

PRAYER POINTS - REVIVAL, INTERCESSION & NATION

1. Father, let revival start with me. Not just in public gatherings, but deep in the secret places of my heart. Wilt Thou not revive us again, that Your people may rejoice in You? (Psalm 85:6)

2. Make me a faithful watchman over my city. Set me upon the walls of my generation - awake, alert, and unrelenting in intercession. I will not hold my peace, day or night (Isaiah 62:6).

3. Heal our land, Lord. Begin the healing in me. As I humble myself and seek Your face, let Heaven respond with mercy and renewal (2 Chronicles 7:14).

4. Awaken the hearts of men in my generation. The harvest is plenteous, but the laborers are few. Make me one of them, faithful and unafraid (Matthew 9:37).

5. Let the fire of Your Spirit burn again across this city and beyond. Empower us by the Holy Ghost to be bold witnesses in every place (Acts 1:8).

6. Protect our sons from the snares of a confused culture. Let them cleanse their way by taking heed to Your Word, and raise them in purity and power (Psalm 119:9).

7. Raise leaders who fear You, seek justice, and uphold truth. Righteousness exalts a nation. May it rise again in our land (Proverbs 14:34).

8. Unseat every throne of spiritual wickedness in high places. For we wrestle not against flesh and blood, but against principalities and powers. Grant us victory in prayer (Ephesians 6:12).

9. Let the Church arise, not in performance, but in power. Build Your Church upon the Rock, and let the gates of hell not prevail against it (Matthew 16:18).

10. Turn the hearts of the fathers to the children, and the hearts of the children to their fathers. Restore the generations and let our sons and daughters prophesy again (Malachi 4:6).

CHAPTER 9

WHEN STRONG ISN'T ENOUGH

A Letter to Men on Emotional Healing & Inner Restoration

Dear Brother,

Strength isn't always about how much you carry; it's also about knowing *when to let go*. There's a silent epidemic among men: smiling on the outside, while bleeding within.

From childhood, many of us were told: "Don't cry," "Man up," "Shake it off." So we learned to suppress pain instead of surrendering to it. We learned how to build walls, but not how to heal what's behind them.

But emotional wounds don't fade because we ignore them. They fester when they stay hidden. God doesn't ask you to toughen up; rather, He invites you to *open up*.

Let me tell you about Kojo's **"healing that started with a sigh."**

Kojo was the dependable one. A father of three, a deacon at his church, and the kind of guy others leaned on in a crisis. But few knew he was unraveling inside. Years of childhood neglect, the sudden death of a sibling, and a betrayal in his marriage had built a quiet storm in his soul.

He didn't scream. He just got quieter.

One evening after Bible study, an older brother pulled him aside and asked, *"When was the last time you cried?"* Kojo chuckled, deflected. But that question haunted him.

The next morning, sitting in his parked car before work, Kojo finally whispered aloud to God, "I'm not okay." And for the first time in 20 years, he let himself cry. In that moment, something broke, and something beautiful began. \

It didn't all change overnight. But that honest prayer became the gate to healing: counseling, authentic friendships, deeper worship, and for the first time, peace that didn't come from pretending.

Today, Kojo leads a support group for men. His scars became testimonies, and his silence gave way to strength.

Brother, God cares about your soul, not just your service.

> *"He healeth the broken in heart, and bindeth up their wounds."* - Psalm 147:3 (KJV).

> *"Cast thy burden upon the Lord, and he shall sustain thee..."* - Psalm 55:22 (KJV).

"The spirit of a man will sustain his infirmity; but a wounded spirit who can bear?"
- Proverbs 18:14 (KJV).

You can't pour from an empty well. You can't lead others while bleeding silently.

Healing doesn't mean weakness; it means humility. And humility opens the door for the Holy Spirit to restore the fractured places and make you whole again.

Let me share with you some steps toward inner restoration:

- **Name your wound** – What still hurts but hasn't been spoken aloud?

- **Take it to God** – Not just as a general prayer, but a specific surrender.

- **Talk to someone** – Healing flows in a safe community (James 5:16).

- **Don't rush the process** – God works slowly in deep places.

- **Remember you're worth restoring** – Not because of what you've done, but because of who He is.

As you reflect on these words, find a quiet, comfortable space and lift these prayers from your heart. Know that you are not alone; many men across the world are kneeling with you to journey towards emotional healing and inner restoration.

PRAYER POINTS - EMOTIONAL HEALING & INNER RESTORATION

1. Father, I bring before You the wounds I've buried deep, the ones I've hidden from others and even tried to hide from myself. Heal my broken heart and bind up every part of me that has been bruised and left unattended (Psalm 147:3).

2. When my heart is overwhelmed and my soul feels crushed under life's weight, lead me to the Rock that is higher than I. You are my refuge and steady place (Psalm 61:2).

3. Where sorrow has sat for years, restore joy to my soul. Though weeping endures for a night, I believe joy comes in the morning. Let laughter return where there was once only silence (Psalm 30:5).

4. Pour peace over my anxious thoughts. Quiet the storm within and keep me in perfect peace as my mind is stayed on You. I fix my focus on Your truth, not my fears (Isaiah 26:3).

5. Replace bitterness with blessing and heaviness with joy. I release resentment and open my heart to wholeness. Let every root of anger, wrath, and pain be uprooted and cast away (Ephesians 4:31).

6. Let forgiveness unlock the freedom I've longed for. Not just toward others, but also toward myself.

Teach me to extend the same mercy I've received. Let kindness and compassion flow through me like healing oil (Ephesians 4:32).

7. I choose to forgive myself and move forward in grace. In Christ, I am a new creation; old things have passed away and all things are becoming new (2 Corinthians 5:17).

8. I receive beauty for ashes today. Where there was mourning, give me gladness. Where there was heaviness, clothe me in praise. Let the oil of joy replace the ache of grief (Isaiah 61:3).

9. Break the silence of shame in my life. I shall not be ashamed, nor hang my head in regret. Instead, I will rejoice in my portion and walk boldly in the covering of Your grace (Isaiah 61:7).

10. Renew hope in the barren places. Where disappointment has lingered, let fresh dreams be born. Hope deferred made my heart sick, but I believe You are birthing desires fulfilled, giving, fruitful, and full of promise (Proverbs 13:12).

CHAPTER 10

THE MAN WHO STOOD AT THE GATE

A Letter to Men on Protection, Covering & Warfare

Dear Brother,

Every home has a roof. Every nation has borders. Every man has a battlefield.

Whether we acknowledge it or not, we are called as protectors of our homes, our hearts, our community, and our spiritual territory. Covering isn't just what we offer others; it's who we become when we take our place on the wall and refuse to back down.

Let me share with you the transformative story of Ernest: **"The Quiet Warrior."**

Ernest was a retired firefighter, a husband, father of two, and elder at his local church. He was neither loud nor seeking applause, but was **present,** especially in prayer.

Every morning at 4:30 a.m., before his wife or kids stirred, he'd walk the perimeter of their house, praying aloud. He'd lay hands on the doorposts, declaring safety over his wife. He'd whisper scriptures over the bedrooms of his children. He called it "circling the camp." To him, it wasn't superstition, but rather *spiritual warfare*.

One night, a car spun out on their street and crashed through the fence, stopping inches from their home. Nobody was hurt. When the family rushed outside, his daughter gasped and said, "It stopped *right* where Dad prays every morning."

To them, it was a coincidence. But to Ernest, it was confirmation.

He never stopped circling the camp. Not just physically, but spiritually - over decisions, ministry, and men in his circle. To this day, the young men at his church still hold him in high esteem."

Brother, here is our warfare role as men, according to the Bible:

"The angel of the Lord encampeth round about them that fear him, and delivereth them."
- Psalm 34:7 (KJV).

"Put on the whole armour of God, that ye may be able to stand against the wiles of the devil."
- Ephesians 6:11 (KJV).

"And I sought for a man among them, that should make up the hedge, and stand in the gap..."
- Ezekiel 22:30 (KJV).

You don't need a title to be a warrior; you just need position and posture - ready to stand, shield in hand, and refusing to let the enemy trespass.

Dear Brother, what will this look like today?

- **Pray for protection daily** - over your family, your brothers, and your city.

- **Discern the gates** - what comes into your home, what voices fill your atmosphere, what seeds are being sown in your children.

- **Be spiritually armed** - know the Word. Put on the armor. Refuse to sleep at the gate.

- **Stand for the vulnerable** - your role as a protector includes the overlooked, the weak, and those still becoming.

As you reflect on these words, find a quiet, comfortable space and lift these prayers from your heart. Know that you are not alone; many men across the world are kneeling with you to understand protection, covering and warfare.

PRAYER POINTS - PROTECTION, COVERING & WARFARE

1. Lord, I come under Your covering today, not in fear, but in faith. You are my shield and my hiding place. Cover me and my household under Your wings, for under Your feathers we find refuge and trust (Psalm 91:4).

2. Let every evil assignment fashioned against me and my family fail. No weapon formed against us shall prosper, and every tongue that rises in judgment, You will condemn. This is my heritage in Christ (Isaiah 54:17).

3. Guard my soul from spiritual ambush. Help me to be sober and vigilant, because the adversary roams, seeking whom to devour. But I stand alert, anchored in Your Word and under Your authority (1 Peter 5:8).

4. Strengthen me to stand firm in the face of spiritual warfare. I draw strength, not from my ability, but from Your power and might. I will not cower in battle, for I am rooted in Your truth (Ephesians 6:10).

5. Dispatch Your angelic hosts to surround and protect me. Let them encamp round about all who fear You and deliver us from every unseen danger. Thank You for divine security beyond what I can see (Psalm 34:7).

6. I cancel every generational curse in my bloodline. I am not bound by patterns of pain or inherited bondage, for Christ has redeemed me from the curse of the law by becoming a curse for me (Galatians 3:13).

7. Let Your truth be my shield and buckler. I will not fight with human weapons, but with the Word of God that pierces darkness and defends my destiny (Psalm 91:4).

8. Today, I put on the whole armor of God: the belt of truth, the breastplate of righteousness, the shield of faith, the helmet of salvation, and the sword of the Spirit. I stand ready and equipped for battle (Ephesians 6:11).

9. Send forth Your light ahead of me in every battle I face. Fight for me as You did for Israel at the Red Sea. I hold my peace while You war on my behalf (Exodus 14:14).

10. May Your presence be a wall of fire around me and my household. Surround us with Your glory. Seal every door the enemy might use to gain access, and let Your Spirit dwell richly within our borders (Zechariah 2:5).

CHAPTER 11

GRATEFUL ANYWAY

A Letter to Men on Gratitude, Praise & Faith

Dear Brother,

Sometimes it's easy to praise God when life is good - when the bills are paid, the doors are open, and the family is smiling. But *true faith* shows up when everything doesn't make sense, and you still lift your eyes and say, *"Thank You, Lord."*

Gratitude isn't just a response; it's a weapon. And praise isn't just noise; it's power.

Let me tell you the compelling story of Kyle's **"praise in the pit."**

Kyle was a small business owner in his 40s who lost nearly everything during a financial collapse: his store, savings, and nearly his faith. The night he packed the final boxes and locked his shop for good, he sat in the driver's seat of his old car and began to cry. He didn't have the words to pray, so he just played worship music.

One lyric stirred something in him: *"I still have breath in my lungs so I'll bless the Lord."* He sat up straight. And right there in that parked car, Kyle lifted his hands and began to thank God not for the loss, but in the midst of it.

The next day, he wrote down everything he still had: a wife who believed in him, kids who still laughed when he came home, and a God who hadn't left him. From that place, gratitude bloomed.

It didn't change overnight, but his faith grew stronger. Two years later, Kyle didn't just rebuild a business; rather, he helped start a men's ministry that's teaching others how to worship from the valley floor.

Here's the meaning of gratitude through the lens of the Word of God:

"In everything, give thanks: for this is the will of God in Christ Jesus concerning you."
- 1 Thessalonians 5:18 (KJV).

"I will bless the Lord at all times: his praise shall continually be in my mouth." - Psalm 34:1 (KJV).

"Now faith is the substance of things hoped for, the evidence of things not seen." - Hebrews 11:1 (KJV).

Praise isn't denial; it's defiance. It tells your problems

that God is still bigger. Gratitude is your declaration that *this valley will not get the last word.*

So, Brother, how can you walk it out?

- **Start small** - Thank God for breath, shelter, memory, mercy. Let thankfulness outpace your complaints.

- **Sing it out** - Turn on worship even when you don't feel like it. Praise until your spirit catches up.

- **Speak Scripture** - Declare promises even when circumstances haven't shifted.

- **Remember the last breakthrough** - If He did it before, He can do it again.

As you reflect on these words, find a quiet, comfortable space and lift these prayers from your heart. Know that you are not alone; many men across the world are kneeling with you to journey towards gratitude, praise and faith.

PRAYER POINTS - GRATITUDE, PRAISE & FAITH

1. Lord, I thank You, not just for the victories, but for Your presence in the valleys. You are good, and Your mercy endures forever. I will give thanks to You in every season (Psalm 107:1).

2. Let my heart overflow with praise. Even when my soul is weary, I will bless the Lord at all times. Your praise shall continually be in my mouth (Psalm 34:1).

3. Teach me to be grateful, even in hardship. I choose to give thanks in everything, not because all things are easy, but because You are faithful in all things (1 Thessalonians 5:18).

4. Open my eyes to daily blessings; food on the table, breath in my lungs, peace amid pressure, and joy in unlikely places. Blessed be the Lord, who daily loads me with benefits (Psalm 68:19).

5. Help me trust even when I cannot trace You. When I do not understand what You are doing, I will still walk by faith, not by sight. My confidence is in You (2 Corinthians 5:7).

6. Let me rest in Your promises. When anxiety rises, remind me that faith is the substance of things hoped for and the evidence of things not seen (Hebrews 11:1).

7. Like Abraham, let me not stagger at what You've promised through unbelief, but grow strong in faith, giving glory to You and standing firm in trust (Romans 4:20).

8. Strengthen my faith until mountains move. If faith as small as a mustard seed can shift the impossible, then let that seed take root in me today (Matthew 17:20).

9. Let my gratitude draw heaven close. I refuse to be anxious for anything, but in everything with thanksgiving. I present my requests to You, trusting in Your peace (Philippians 4:6).

10. Thank You for giving me victory through Christ Jesus. Let my worship silence every worry, and let my song unlock joy that circumstances cannot take away (1 Corinthians 15:57).

CHAPTER 12

YOUR NAME AFTER YOU

A Letter to Men on Legacy, Impact & Blessing Generations

Dear Brother,

Legacy is not what we leave *for* people; it's what we leave in them.

It's not just money, land, or reputation; it's faith handed down and values embedded in bloodlines, and truth whispered in kitchens, shouted in prayer closets, and written into how we live every day.

You are a bridge between the past and the future. *They* will walk on what you build today, tomorrow.

Let me share a story with you about **"Mr. Isaac's chair."**

Every Sunday after church, Mr. Isaac, a retired teacher in his 70s, would sit in the same wooden chair outside his porch. Without fail, one or two of his grown sons, and often a grandson, would come to sit with him.

He didn't say much. He just told short stories, quoted scriptures like *"The memory of the just is blessed"* (Proverbs 10:7), and sometimes asked simple, piercing questions like, *"Who are you becoming?"*

When he passed, his family had his chair carefully restored and kept on that same porch.

Now his oldest grandson, Felix, sits in it every Sunday, reading Proverbs to his nieces and nephews, passing on wisdom his grandfather first deposited.

That old chair became more than furniture; it became an altar of legacy.

Below are some biblical truths about generational blessings

"A good man leaveth an inheritance to his children's children..." - Proverbs 13:22 (KJV).

"His seed shall be mighty upon earth: The generation of the upright shall be blessed." - Psalm 112:2 (KJV).

"That the generation to come might know them... and might set their hope in God." - Psalm 78:6–7 (KJV).

You are not just a man of this moment; you are a man of multiplication. Heaven doesn't measure your success by what you accumulate, but by what you deposit, and who still walks faithfully because *you did*.

Finally, these are steps on how you can build a legacy today:

- **Model what you want remembered** – Your children will forget your speeches, but never your example.

- **Speak blessing intentionally** – Don't assume they know. Tell them who they are in God's eyes.

- **Live with eternity in view** – Check within - What seeds are you sowing that will outlive you?

- **Invest in more than your own** – Legacy multiplies when you bless those who may never carry your name, but will carry your wisdom.

- As you reflect on these words, find a quiet, comfortable space and lift these prayers from your heart. Know that you are not alone; many men across the world are kneeling with you to make impact and be a blessing beyond our generation.

PRAYER POINTS - LEGACY, IMPACT & BLESSING FUTURE GENERATIONS

1. Father, may my life leave a trail of light for those who come behind me. Teach me to pour what I've received into faithful men, so they too may teach others. Let generational impact begin with me (2 Timothy 2:2).

2. Let my legacy be spiritual, not just material. I don't want to merely leave behind wealth. I want to leave behind wisdom, worship, and a witness that echoes for eternity (Proverbs 13:22).

3. Let my name carry honor in both heaven and on earth. A good name is to be chosen over great riches, and I desire that my name be remembered for truth, for love, and for walking with You (Proverbs 22:1).

4. Use my testimony to break chains and open doors for others. Let the story of my deliverance be the key to someone else's breakthrough. We overcome by the blood and by the word of our testimony (Revelation 12:11).

5. Help me disciple the next generation with patience, purpose, and power. Let me go, teach, and model Christ so others can walk in His fullness (Matthew 28:19).

6. Let the fire in me never go out. Fan the flame of devotion until the altar of my life is never without incense. Keep me burning with holy passion until the very end (Leviticus 6:13).

7. Let my family line be marked by righteousness. May my children, and their children, know integrity not just by hearing it taught but by watching it lived out. Let our generation be blessed (Psalm 112:2).

8. Let my memory be a blessing. When my name is spoken, may it stir faith and not fear, hope and not pain. Let the memory of the just remain fragrant in generations to come (Proverbs 10:7).

9. Make my name great, not by ambition or pride, but by Your own hand so that I may be a blessing to many. Use me as a vessel of generational impact (Genesis 12:2).

10. Keep me faithful to the very end. Let me run my race well. And when I am gone, may the path behind me be clear, the standard unshaken, and the legacy lasting, unto a crown of life (Revelation 2:10).

CHAPTER 13

FAITH, BUDGET, AND THE BROKE SEASON

A Letter to Men on Financial Stability, Provision, and Contentment

Dear Brother,

Financial stability doesn't begin in a bank account; it starts in a heart aligned with wisdom, humility, and trust in God. Yes, we need plans, discipline, and hustle. But, before all of that, we need the convictions that: **money is a tool, not our identity, and p**rovision is a promise, not a god.

Here's a story every man needs to hear - **"Tunde and the Envelope Testimony"**

Tunde was a youth pastor and part-time delivery driver. After his father passed, he became the primary provider for his younger siblings. Tunde was passionate but underpaid. One month, with rent looming and only

$87 in his account, he stood in church while the offering basket passed and whispered, *"God, I trust You, but I don't even know what obedience looks like right now."*

He felt prompted to give, not out of pressure, but peace. He placed a $20 bill into the offering and wrote three things on the envelope: **"Wisdom. Open doors. No shame."**

By the end of that week, he received a call from a friend he hadn't spoken to in years, offering him a media work contract for a local nonprofit. The job opened up a steady income.

The burden lessened. But here's the real breakthrough: his mindset shifted. Tunde began tracking every expense, setting weekly saving goals, and teaching his siblings how to plan with purpose.

Now, years later, he doesn't boast about how much he makes; he shares how **freedom came from faith, structure, and stewardship.**

Let me share with you Biblical perspectives on financial principles

"The blessing of the Lord, it maketh rich, and he addeth no sorrow with it." - Proverbs 10:22 (KJV).

"Be thou diligent to know the state of thy flocks, and look well to thy herds." - Proverbs 27:23 (KJV).

"Moreover it is required in stewards that a man be found faithful." - 1 Corinthians 4:2 (KJV).

Financial stability is not just about income; it's about **integrity**, **intentionality**, and **obedience**. God's desire is not just to increase your finances but to enlarge your wisdom with them.

Finally, these are practical takeaways for the financially faithful man:

- **Know where your money goes.** Track it, steward it, and assign it purposefully.

- **Tithe and give, even in lean seasons.** Giving anchors your heart in God, not mammon.

- **Build margin slowly.** Small savings consistently beat emotional spending.

- **Ask for wisdom, not just provision.** God's strategy often precedes His supply.

- **Talk about it.** Don't suffer financial stress in silence. Find a mentor or group that can walk with you.

As you reflect on these words, find a quiet, comfortable space and lift these prayers from your heart. Know that you are not alone; many men across the world are kneeling with you to journey towards financial stability, provision and contentment.

PRAYER POINTS – FINANCIAL STABILITY, PROVISION & CONTENTMENT

1. Father, You are my Shepherd, I shall not want. I trust You to provide for my family and meet every unseen need, for You shall supply all my needs according to Your riches in glory (Psalm 23:1; Philippians 4:19).

2. You are my Source, my Provider in all things. I renounce anxiety and fear concerning provision. I choose rest, because my supply is rooted in Your abundance, not my striving (Psalm 23:1).

3. Teach me to honor You with my substance. Let my finances reflect worship and obedience. I refuse to let money govern my decisions. May my giving glorify You, not impress others (Proverbs 3:9).

4. Let my prosperity be rooted in Your blessing alone. I don't chase riches, I seek righteousness. Prosper me in a way that adds no sorrow, for the blessing of the Lord makes rich (Proverbs 10:22).

5. Build deep contentment in my heart. Whether I have much or little, teach me to say with Paul: "I have learned to be content" (Philippians 4:11). Keep my soul at rest, even when my hands are busy.

6. Help me steward resources with legacy and impact in mind. A good man leaves an inheritance to his children's children. May I think beyond myself and build for generations to come (Proverbs 13:22).

7. Form in me financial integrity. Whether in plenty or in lack, make me faithful with what I have. Let me be counted trustworthy even in the smallest things (Luke 16:10).

8. Let my priorities be spiritual before financial. I choose to seek first Your Kingdom, knowing that every other need will be added as I align my life with Your will (Matthew 6:33).

9. Make me a joyful giver. I will not withhold out of fear. I give generously, knowing it shall be given back to me, pressed down, shaken together, and running over (Luke 6:38).

10. Let me refresh others and be refreshed in return. The liberal soul shall be made fat; he that waters others shall be watered also. Use me as a vessel of provision, grace, and generosity (Proverbs 11:25).

CHAPTER 14

EYES UP, FEET FORWARD

A Letter to Men on Vision, Calling & Direction

Dear Brother,

We all reach that place: a crossroads where what we *see* doesn't match what we *sense*. The path is unclear, and the pressure to make something of our lives weighs heavily.

Calling isn't found in a spotlight; it's revealed in surrender. Direction doesn't begin with a roadmap; it begins with trust in the One who sees farther than we do.

Let me tell you about David - not the one from Scripture, but a modern brother whose story may echo yours - **"The Detour that Wasn't."**

David was a trained architect, talented, and driven. Three years into building his dream firm, out of nowhere, client fallout led to financial collapse. He tried salvaging what he could, but within months, he had to let go of his staff, sell his car, and work part-time at a hardware store to stay afloat.

One night after closing, he was shelving paint cans when an elderly customer asked if he knew anything about restoring old porches. He hesitated, but then said yes.

That simple repair turned into a side project. Soon, David was flooded with requests from clients who didn't just want structures but spaces restored with heart. Without realizing it, he'd stepped into a new calling: *restoration architect.*

Years later, he now runs a successful nonprofit that helps single mothers and veterans renovate their homes. He still draws and designs, but now, it's fueled by **vision**, not ego.

David thought the detour ended his purpose. But God saw it as the beginning.

Here are some scriptures for the journey:

"The steps of a good man are ordered by the Lord: and he delighteth in his way." - Psalm 37:23 (KJV).

"A man's heart deviseth his way: but the Lord directeth his steps." - Proverbs 16:9 (KJV).

"I press toward the mark for the prize of the high calling of God in Christ Jesus." - Philippians 3:14 (KJV).

You don't have to see the full staircase. Just take the next step.

Here are ways to move with vision and direction:

- **Start where you are** - God often speaks while you're moving, not just when you're waiting.

- **Stay faithful in the small** - Vision is built one act of obedience at a time.

- **Silence the noise** - If everyone is pulling at your time, spend more of it with the One who called you.

- **Measure success by alignment, not applause** - Is this God's way, or just a good idea?

As you reflect on these words, find a quiet, comfortable space and lift these prayers from your heart. Know that you are not alone; many men across the world are kneeling with you to discover our vision, calling and direction.

PRAYER POINTS –
VISION, CALLING & DIRECTION

1. Father, I lift my eyes to You, the Author and Finisher of my journey. Order my steps, Lord. Let me walk in Your will today, not led by impulse, but by divine alignment (Psalm 37:23).

2. Even when I don't see the full picture, I trust Your plan. You know the thoughts You think toward me

- thoughts of peace, not of evil, to give me a future filled with hope (Jeremiah 29:11).

3. I acknowledge You in all my ways. Direct my paths. Guide my journey with divine direction and let every part of my life come under the influence of Your counsel and grace (Proverbs 3:6).

4. Align my plans with Your eternal purpose. I surrender every idea and ambition to the wisdom of heaven. There are many plans in a man's heart, but only Your counsel shall stand (Proverbs 19:21).

5. Let Your Word shine over every decision I make. Be a lamp unto my feet and a light unto my path. May I never walk in darkness or confusion, but always in the clarity of Your truth (Psalm 119:105).

6. Strengthen me to keep pressing forward with relentless focus. I refuse distractions and delays. I press toward the mark for the prize of the high calling in Christ Jesus (Philippians 3:14).

7. Keep my eyes fixed on You. Let me not be moved by detours or detractions. I will look straight ahead, with vision sharpened and purpose refined (Proverbs 4:25).

8. Redirect me when necessary. When my plans fail or my path seems blocked, remind me that a man may devise his way, but it is the Lord who directs his steps (Proverbs 16:9).

9. Perfect the good work You've started in me. You do not abandon assignments midway. I rest in Your mercy and believe that You will complete what concerns me (Psalm 138:8).

10. I call on You for vision beyond my natural sight and wisdom beyond my understanding. Answer me, Lord. Reveal great and mighty things I do not yet know, and let my life be led by revelation, not just reason (Jeremiah 33:3).

CHAPTER 15

BUILD WHAT GOD BREATHED

A Letter to Men on Kingdom Entrepreneurship

Dear Brother,

Entrepreneurship is more than making money; it's responding to a **divine assignment** to build, create, and solve real problems on earth. God didn't give you vision to impress; He gave it to you so you could *impact*.

None of the business ideas, skills in your hands, and every door that closes is random. Kingdom entrepreneurs don't just chase profits; they carry purpose.

Let me introduce you to someone who understood that - **"Jide and the Barber Chair That Turned Into a Movement."**

Jide started as a street-side barber with a secondhand chair and a $40 clipper. No branding. No storefront - just a cardboard sign that read "Cuts - Walk In. Talk Life."

He wasn't the most gifted, but he listened. While cutting hair, he'd speak life into young boys struggling with school, encourage dads fighting silent battles, and pray quietly over every customer.

One afternoon, a man, an HR director who was going through depression, came in for a 20-minute haircut, which became a divine encounter. Afterward, the man said, "This was more than a cut. You restored my strength."

That moment gave Jide a new revelation: he wasn't building a business; he was **building a platform for healing.** Three years later, the place is now a mentorship hub with staff trained not just in fades, but in **faith.**

Brother, here is what the word of God says about builders like you:

> *"Seest thou a man diligent in his business? he shall stand before kings; he shall not stand before mean men."* - Proverbs 22:29 (KJV).

> *"Commit thy works unto the Lord, and thy thoughts shall be established."* - Proverbs 16:3 (KJV).

> *"I have filled him with the spirit of God... in all manner of workmanship."* - Exodus 31:3 (KJV).

God is not just in the pulpit; He's in the blueprint. He's not just anointing preachers; He's empowering *builders, consultants, barbers, tailors, and tech founders* - You.

Finally, these are nuggets and wisdom for kingdom entrepreneurs:

- **Start with vision, stay with discipline** - Passion ignites; structure sustains.

- **Solve problems, not just sell products** - People follow what heals them.

- **Don't underestimate small beginnings** - Obedience is often disguised as obscurity.

- **Let prayer lead strategy** - Devotion before expansion.

As you reflect on these words, find a quiet, comfortable space and lift these prayers from your heart. Know that you are not alone; many men across the world are kneeling with you to unravel kingdom entrepreneurship.

PRAYER POINTS – KINGDOM ENTREPRENEURSHIP

1. Father, I dedicate my entrepreneurial journey to You. I commit my works into Your hands. Breathe on every idea You've planted in my spirit. Establish my steps and anchor my plans in Your wisdom and will (Proverbs 16:3).

2. Grant me wisdom to make decisions that honor You and lead to true success. When I lack direction, remind me that You give liberally to those who ask without reproach (James 1:5).

3. Teach me to labor with diligence and integrity, not for applause but because You reward faithfulness. Let my excellence speak for me and bring me before kings (Proverbs 22:29).

4. Align my business pursuits with Your kingdom purpose. Let seeking You be my first instinct, not an afterthought. As I put You first, let all other things be added in divine order (Matthew 6:33).

5. Establish the work of my hands and let it bear fruit that brings You glory. May Your beauty rest upon every project I build, and may it reflect the fragrance of heaven (Psalm 90:17).

6. Silence every fear that tries to hold me back. Where doubt and hesitation lurk, fill me with courage and boldness. I receive power, love, and a sound mind for this assignment (2 Timothy 1:7).

7. Teach me to manage my time, talent, and treasure with wisdom. Help me steward both the small and the great faithfully, knowing that trust is proven in both (1 Corinthians 4:2).

8. Let people always come before profit. Fill my heart with compassion, not competition. Let my business be known for service, humility, and integrity (Philippians 2:3).

9. May my work shine as a testimony of Your goodness. Let every client, partner, or staff encounter the light of Christ through my actions and decisions (Matthew 5:16).

10. And when I'm gone, let what I built still speak. Make my business a legacy that blesses generations and a work rooted in faith, obedience, and impact (Proverbs 13:22).

CHAPTER 16

THE SILENT ROOM

A Letter to Men on Solitude, Reflection & Hearing God Clearly

Dear Brother,

There's a room every man must enter if he wants to truly hear God. It's not a physical space; rather, it's a posture of the heart. It's the place where noise fades, distractions die, and the voice of the Father becomes unmistakable.

But let's be honest: silence can be uncomfortable. For many of us, it feels like weakness. We're used to fixing things, solving problems, and staying busy. Sitting still feels unproductive. Yet, it's in the silent room that God does His deepest work.

Let's hear the story of **"Samuel's Turning Point in Solitude."**

Years ago, a man named Samuel was at a crossroads in his life. He was a successful engineer, a husband, and a father, but inside, he felt empty. The pressures of work, family, and ministry were pulling him in every direction, and he couldn't hear God's voice anymore.

One day, Samuel decided to take a weekend retreat alone. He rented a small cabin in the woods, turned off his phone, and brought only his Bible and a journal. At first, the silence was deafening. He felt restless, tempted to check emails or call home. But as the hours passed, something shifted.

In the stillness, Samuel began to pour out his heart to God - his fears, frustrations, and failures. He read **Psalm 46:10**: *"Be still, and know that I am God."* Slowly, the noise in his mind quieted, and he felt God's presence like never before.

By the end of the weekend, Samuel had clarity about his next steps. He realized he needed to prioritize his family over his career and trust God with the uncertainties ahead. That silent room became the turning point in his life.

Here are Biblical points of view on solitude and hearing God clearly:

"Be still, and know that I am God: I will be exalted among the heathen, I will be exalted in the earth."
– Psalms 46:10 (KJV).

"And Jacob was left alone; and there wrestled a man with him until the breaking of the day."
– Genesis 32:24 (KJV).

"And in the morning, rising up a great while before day,
he went out, and departed into a solitary place, and there
prayed." – Mark 1:35 (KJV).

So, Brother, why do men need the silent room?

- **To Hear God's Voice -** The world is loud, but God speaks in whispers. Solitude helps us tune out distractions and focus on His Word.

- **To Reflect on Our Lives -** Silence gives us space to evaluate our priorities, decisions, and direction. It's where we ask, "Am I living for God or myself?"

- **To Renew Our Strength** - Isaiah 40:31 reminds us that those who wait on the Lord will renew their strength. The silent room is where we wait, listen, and receive.

- **To Surrender Control** - In solitude, we let go of the need to fix everything and trust God to lead us.

The silent room is where clarity is born. It's where God reminds us who we are, refines our vision, and restores our strength. It's where we stop striving and start surrendering.

The silent room is not a place of weakness; it's a place of strength. It's where men meet God, wrestle with their fears, and rise with renewed purpose. Don't be afraid to enter it. In the stillness, you'll find the clarity, peace, and power you've been searching for.

Let's kneel in the silent room and listen as God speaks.

As you reflect on these words, find a quiet, comfortable space and lift these prayers from your heart. Know that you are not alone; many men across the world are kneeling with you in quiet reflection to hear God more clearly.

PRAYER POINTS – SOLITUDE, REFLECTION & HEARING GOD CLEARLY

1. Lord, teach me to be still and to know that You are God. Stillness is not emptiness; it's a sacred posture where You are exalted above the noise and lifted high above my striving (Psalm 46:10).

2. Open my ears to hear Your voice clearly in the quiet. I am one of Your sheep, and I choose to follow, not just when the path is clear, but even when all I have is the sound of Your whisper (John 10:27).

3. As I wait on You, renew my strength. Lift me above discouragement and fatigue. Cause me to mount up with wings like an eagle - strong, focused, and free (Isaiah 40:31).

4. I surrender every plan I've made without You. I lay them at Your feet and trust You to direct my path, even when the way seems uncertain (Proverbs 3:5-6).

5. Fill my heart with the kind of peace that doesn't make sense to the world, peace that passes understanding, anchoring my heart and mind in Christ (Philippians 4:7).

6. Grant me wisdom, Lord. Let clarity rise where confusion once reigned. I ask boldly, because You give generously to those who seek You (James 1:5).

7. Create in me a clean heart. If there's anything in me that blocks Your voice or clouds Your presence, purge it. Renew a right spirit within me - one that is tender, humble, and yielded (Psalm 51:10).

8. Guide me, Father. Instruct me in the way I should go and watch over every step I take. Let me walk in rhythm with Your eye and not miss my moment (Psalm 32:8).

9. Give me the courage to obey, especially when the instruction stretches me. Let my boldness be rooted not in self-confidence, but in the assurance that You are with me wherever I go (Joshua 1:9).

10. Draw me close in every quiet moment. Let the silence become a sanctuary. In stillness, speak. In solitude, sanctify. And in reflection, reform me. I draw near to You, knowing You are drawing near to me (James 4:8).

CHAPTER 17

———— ❧ ————

THE FATHER'S WOUND

A Letter to Men Healing from Absent or Hurting Fathers

Dear Brother,

Every man carries a story about his father. For some, it's a story of love, strength, and affirmation. For others, it's a story of absence, rejection, or pain. The father wound is one of the deepest wounds a man can carry. It shapes how he sees himself, relates to others, and even how he views God.

If your father was absent, you may wrestle with feelings of abandonment or inadequacy. If your father was harsh or unloving, you may struggle with anger, resentment, or a fear of failure. These wounds don't just disappear with time; they linger in the shadows of our hearts, influencing our choices and relationships.

Let's hear Daniel's story of transformation **"From Anger to Healing"**.

Daniel grew up in a single-parent home. His father left when he was five years old, and Daniel spent most of his childhood wondering why he wasn't enough for his dad to stay. As he grew older, that pain turned into anger. He vowed never to be like his father, but the wound still controlled him.

In his twenties, Daniel became a father himself. He loved his children deeply, but he found himself repeating patterns he hated - being emotionally distant and quick to anger. One day, after an argument with his wife, Daniel broke down. He realized he was still carrying the pain of his father's absence.

He began to seek healing by joining a men's group at church, where he shared his story for the first time. He also spent time in prayer, asking God to help him forgive his father and heal his heart. Slowly, Daniel felt the weight lifted. He began to see himself not as a victim of his father's choices, but as a son of God - loved, valued, and whole.

Today, Daniel is a different man. He's intentional about being present for his children and showing them the love he never received. His story is proof that God can redeem even the deepest wounds.

Here are Biblical points of view on healing from impact of absent fathers:

> *"When my father and my mother forsake me, then the Lord will take me up."* – Psalsms 27:10 (KJV).

81

"But when he was yet a great way off, his father saw him, and had compassion..." - Luke 15:20 (KJV).

"Therefore if any man be in Christ, he is a new creature: old things are passed away; behold, all things are become new." - 2 Corinthians 5:17 (KJV).

Brother, here are the steps toward healing:

- **Acknowledge the Pain** - Healing begins with honesty. Admit the hurt and allow yourself to grieve.

- **Forgive Your Father** - Forgiveness doesn't excuse the wrong; it frees you from its grip.

- **Embrace Your Identity in Christ** - You are not defined by your father's actions; you are a son of God, loved and chosen.

- **Seek Community** - Surround yourself with men who will encourage and support your healing journey.

- **Let God Be Your Father** - God is the perfect Father who will never leave or forsake you.

But here's the truth: healing is possible. No matter how deep the wound, God, the ultimate Father, can restore what was broken. He can fill the void left by an earthly father and remind you of your true identity as His beloved son.

The father's wound is real, but so is God's healing. You don't have to carry the pain forever. Bring it to the One who knows you fully and loves you completely. Let Him fill the void, heal the hurt, and remind you of your worth.

You are not defined by your father's absence or mistakes; you are defined by God's love.

As you reflect on these words, find a quiet, comfortable space and lift these prayers from your heart. Know that you are not alone; many men across the world are kneeling with you to journey towards healing from generational impact of absent and hurting fathers.

PRAYER POINTS – HEALING FROM ABSENT OR HURTING FATHERS

1. Lord, I bring You the pain I've carried for years - the silent ache of absence and the scars of disappointment. You are near to the brokenhearted, and You save those crushed in spirit. You see what others missed, and You hold what I could never express (Psalm 34:18).

2. I release my earthly father from the debt of what he did or failed to do. I choose forgiveness, not because it was easy, but because it's necessary for my healing. I will not be bound by bitterness or imprisoned by blame (Matthew 6:14; Ephesians 4:31).

3. Heal the wounds that shaped me. Speak into the broken places and bind up what life and neglect tore apart. I believe You are restoring me to wholeness - heart, mind, and memory (Psalm 147:3).

4. Remind me daily that I am not fatherless. I am Your beloved son, chosen and deeply loved. I carry Your name. I am not overlooked. I am embraced (1 John 3:1).

5. Lord, free me from the anger I've carried far too long toward my father. Bitterness has clouded my heart and chained my soul. I surrender it to You. Replace resentment with peace, and pain with healing. Teach me to forgive fully, as You have forgiven me (Ephesians 4:31).

6. Fill my heart with peace, Lord. Let it run deeper than my understanding and quiet every emotional storm. Guard my mind from lies and wrap my heart in Your calm (Philippians 4:7).

7. Break the patterns that have run through my family line. I am in Christ. The old has passed away, and all things have become new. I choose to lead my family with love, not with pain (2 Corinthians 5:17).

8. If it is Your will, restore my relationship with my earthly father. Heal the distance. Mend the silence. Turn hearts back to one another, just as You promised (Malachi 4:6).

9. Surround me with godly men who will walk with me - brothers who sharpen me, mentors who pour into me, and friends who speak life (Proverbs 27:17).

10. Teach me to trust You as my perfect Father. You defend the fatherless. You cover me with strength and affection. You are not absent. You are always present and always enough (Psalm 68:5).

CHAPTER 18

FAITH IN THE WILDERNESS

A Letter to Men Navigating Transition, Delay & Waiting Seasons

Dear Brother,

The wilderness is a place no man chooses, yet every man must walk through at some point in his life. It's the space between where you were and where you're going; a season of transition, delay, and waiting. It's where dreams seem distant, prayers feel unanswered, and God's voice seems silent.

But the wilderness is not a punishment; it's a preparation. It's where God refines your character, deepens your faith, and teaches you to trust Him in ways you never have before.

Let me share with you the inspiring story of Jamal – **"The Carpenter and his Waiting Season"**

Jamal was a skilled carpenter with big dreams of starting his own construction business. For years, he worked tirelessly for others, saving every penny and praying for the right opportunity. But every time he thought he was ready, something would go wrong - a deal would fall through, a loan would be denied, or unexpected expenses would drain his savings.

Frustrated and discouraged, Jamal began to question God: "Why am I still here? Haven't I been faithful? When will it be my turn?"

One day, while working on a small project for an elderly widow, Jamal felt God impress something on his heart: *"Be faithful where you are."* He realized he had been so focused on the future that he had neglected the opportunities right in front of him.

Jamal decided to shift his perspective. He started treating every project, no matter how small, as if it were his own business. He built relationships, served his clients with excellence, and trusted God with the timing.

Years later, when the opportunity finally came to start his own company, Jamal was ready, not just financially, but spiritually. The wilderness had taught him patience, humility, and faith. Today, his business is thriving, and he often shares his story to encourage others in their waiting seasons.

Think of Moses, who spent 40 years in the wilderness before leading Israel out of Egypt, or David, who hid in caves before becoming king. Even Jesus was led into the wilderness before beginning His ministry.

Here are Biblical points of view on experiencing wilderness, delays and waiting seasons:

"But he knoweth the way that I take: when he hath tried me, I shall come forth as gold."
– Job 23:10 (KJV)

"To every thing there is a season, and a time to every purpose under the heaven." – Ecclesiastes 3;1 (KJV)

"For the vision is yet for an appointed time… though it tarry, wait for it; because it will surely come, it will not tarry." - Habakkuk 2:3 (KJV).

Finally, here are some lessons from the wilderness:

- **The Wilderness is Temporary** - No season lasts forever. Trust that God is leading you through, not leaving you there.

- **The Wilderness is a Classroom** - God uses this time to teach you lessons you'll need for the next season. Don't waste it.

- **The Wilderness is a Test of Faith** - Will you trust God when you can't see the way forward?

- **The Wilderness is a Place of Provision** - Just as God provided manna for Israel, He will provide for you in unexpected ways.

- **The Wilderness Prepares You for the Promise** - What God has for you is worth the wait.

The wilderness is not the end of your story; rather, it's the training ground for your next chapter. It's the beginning of something greater. Trust that God is with you, even when He feels distant. Lean into His Word, stay faithful in the small things, and know that He is preparing you for a promise that is worth the wait.

You are not alone in this season. God is working in you, through you, and for you. Keep the faith.

As you reflect on these words, find a quiet, comfortable space and lift these prayers from your heart. Know that you are not alone; many men across the world are kneeling with you to navigate transitions, delays and waiting seasons.

PRAYER POINTS – NAVIGATING TRANSITION, DELAY & WAITING SEASONS

1. Lord, I choose to trust Your timing, even when I don't understand the delays. To everything there is a season, and this waiting season is not wasted. You are working even in silence (Ecclesiastes 3:1).

2. Give me strength for today. Not to escape the process, but to endure it with faith. Those who wait on You shall renew their strength. Let me rise like an eagle, above weariness and worry (Isaiah 40:31).

3. Lead me through this wilderness, Lord. I refuse to lean on my understanding. I trust You to direct my path, even when the road is unclear (Proverbs 3:5-6).

4. Teach me contentment here. Help me to be faithful in the now - serving, learning, and loving without resentment or restlessness (Philippians 4:11).

5. Just as You provided for Israel, provide for me in this season. Let manna fall if needed. Let water flow from dry places. Supply all my needs according to Your riches in glory (Philippians 4:19).

6. I walk by faith and not by sight. Even when I can't see ahead, I know You are leading. I trust You in the fog, in the silence, in the in-between (2 Corinthians 5:7).

7. Grant me wisdom for every decision - where to go, when to move, and how to wait. You said if I ask, You will give generously, and I believe You will (James 1:5).

8. Shape my heart. If it takes humility to be ready, then humble me under Your mighty hand. Refine my character until it can carry the promise (1 Peter 5:6).

9. Guard my heart with Your peace - the kind that doesn't need all the answers. Quiet every anxious thought and anchor me in calm assurance (Philippians 4:7).

10. And when the time comes, prepare me for what You've promised. I believe You've started something good in me and You will finish it, perfectly, in Your time (Philippians 1:6).

CHAPTER 19

RISING WHILE CARRYING

A Letter to Men Grieving Loss of a Loved One

Dear Brother,

Loss changes you. It doesn't ask for permission, and it doesn't wait for you to be ready. The death of a loved one hits deep like a piercing arrow. Grief comes like an uninvited guest and stays longer than you expect.

As men, we're often taught to carry pain in silence. To "be strong" for others, even when we feel like we're breaking inside. But hear this: **Grief is not weakness.** It's the evidence of love, the weight of what mattered deeply to you.

You don't have to bear the weight of the loss alone.

Let's sit and listen to the story of Nathan – **"The Father Who Lost His Son"**

Nathan was a man of faith, a devoted husband, and a proud father of three. His youngest son, Caleb, was the joy of his life, always laughing and curious. But at just 8 years old, Caleb was diagnosed with leukemia.

For two years, Nathan prayed, fasted, and believed for healing. He held Caleb's hand through every treatment, every sleepless night, and every tear. But on one cold December morning, Caleb took his last breath.

Nathan was shattered. He felt like he had failed as a father, as a protector. He questioned God, asking why his prayers hadn't been answered. At Caleb's funeral, Nathan stood strong for his family, but inside, he felt like he was carrying the coffin of his faith along with his son.

It wasn't until months later, during a quiet moment in prayer, that Nathan heard God whisper: **"You didn't fail. You loved him well."**

Nathan began to see that grief wasn't something to "get over"; it was something to carry with grace. He learned to lean on God in his brokenness, to let trusted friends walk with him, and to honor Caleb's memory by living with purpose. Today, Nathan still misses his son, but carries the coffin differently - not as a burden, but as a testimony of love and hope.

Here are Biblical points of view on grieving loss of loved ones:

"Jesus wept." - John 11:35 (KJV)

"The Lord is nigh unto them that are of a broken heart;
and saveth such as be of a contrite spirit."
- Psalm 34:18 (KJV)

"But I would not have you to be ignorant, brethren,
concerning them which are asleep... that ye sorrow not,
even as others which have no hope."
- 1 Thessalonians 4:13 (KJV)

So, Brother, here are some lessons you can learn from grief:

- **Grief is a Journey, Not a Destination** - Healing doesn't happen overnight. It's okay to take your time.

- **You Don't Have to Be Strong Alone** - Let others walk with you. Vulnerability is not weakness; it's courage.

- **God is Near to the Brokenhearted** - He sees your tears, hears your questions, and holds you in your pain.

- **Your Pain Has Purpose** - It may not make sense now, but God can use your story to bring hope to others.

- **Love Doesn't End with Loss** - The memories, the impact, and the legacy live on.

Healing from grief is not about "getting over it"; it's about learning to live with the loss while allowing God, time, and community to gently restore your heart.

Finally, these are steps you can take to heal from grief:

- **Acknowledge the Pain Honestly**: Don't suppress it. Grief is love that has nowhere to go. Speak, write, and cry it.

- **Permit Yourself to Grieve**: There's no deadline for healing. Let the tears flow. Let the silence speak.

- **Lean into God's Presence:** Grief may feel like abandonment, but God is closest in the valley. Worship, even if it's through tears.

- **Find Safe Community:** Healing often happens in a relationship. Talk to someone who won't rush your process.

- **Honor What Was Lost:** Create memorials, write letters, plant something, or share stories. Let love continue in new ways.

- **Let God Rebuild You:** You may not be the same, but you can be whole again. Let Him reshape your heart.

- **Walk Forward with Purpose:** Grief doesn't erase your calling; it refines it. Let your story become someone else's survival guide.

Grief doesn't mean you've failed; it means you've loved deeply. Rising while carrying the pain of the loss is not about forgetting what you've lost; it's about honoring it with how you live.

God sees your tears, hears your prayers, and walks with you through the valley. You don't have to carry the weight alone. Let Him strengthen you, comfort you, and remind you that even in loss, there is hope.

Your story isn't over; it's being rewritten by the One who makes all things new.

As you reflect on these words, find a quiet, comfortable space and lift these prayers from your heart. Know that you are not alone; many men across the world are kneeling with you and wrapping our arms around you during these difficult times.

PRAYER POINTS – MEN GRIEVING LOSS

1. Lord, I bring my broken heart to You. I feel the weight of this loss more than I can explain. Comfort me in the pain I cannot articulate. You said, *Blessed are those who mourn, for they shall be comforted,* and I believe You will not leave me comfortless (Matthew 5:4).

2. Strengthen me today, Lord. Some days it feels impossible to rise, but You have promised to uphold me with Your righteous right hand. Be near, and help me stand when I feel like falling (Isaiah 41:10).

3. Let Your peace guard my heart. I don't ask for answers, I ask for stillness inside the storm. Give me peace that passes all understanding; peace that holds me when nothing else can (Philippians 4:7).

4. Heal the hidden wounds. I don't want to fake strength; I want to be made whole. Bind up my broken heart and restore my inner man with Your love and presence (Psalm 147:3).

5. Even in the pain I don't understand, help me trust Your plan. Remind me that Your thoughts toward me are good, and that You still have a future filled with peace and purpose for my life (Jeremiah 29:11).

6. Where bitterness has grown in the soil of grief, pull it up, Lord. Teach me how to forgive, not to excuse, but to be free. Let my heart be tender again (Ephesians 4:32).

7. Remind me that this valley is not forever. Hope still lives. I will yet praise You. Speak to my soul until it begins to rise again, and remind me that You are the health of my countenance (Psalm 42:11).

8. Even in this darkness, I know You're with me. Walk beside me in the valley of the shadow of death. Let Your rod and Your staff be my comfort when nothing else can (Psalm 23:4).

9. Restore my joy, Lord. I know joy and grief can walk hand-in-hand. Show me how to laugh again, live again, and breathe again, because the joy of the Lord is my strength (Nehemiah 8:10).

10. Use this story, Lord. Don't let this pain be wasted. Turn it into a purpose. Teach me how to carry the legacy of what I've lost with honor, and let all things - yes, even this - work together for good (Romans 8:28).

CHAPTER 20

THE ROOM CALLED REGRET

A Letter to Men Haunted by Past Mistakes

Dear Brother,

Regret is a heavy room to live in. It's filled with echoes of "What if?" and "If only." The walls are lined with memories you wish you could erase, and the air feels thick with shame.

But here's the truth: **Regret doesn't have to be your prison.**

We all make mistakes - some small and some life-altering. But God's grace is bigger than your worst failure. He doesn't see you as the sum of your mistakes; He sees you as His beloved son, redeemed and restored.

It's time to leave the room called regret and step into the freedom of forgiveness.

Let's lean in on the inspiring story of Fred – **"The Businessman Who Lost Everything"**

Fred was a successful entrepreneur, known for his bold decisions and relentless drive. But one risky investment turned his thriving business into bankruptcy. He lost his company, his savings, and the trust of his family.

For years, Fred lived in the room called regret. He replayed every decision, every warning he ignored, every dollar he lost. He felt like a failure, not just as a businessman, but as a husband and father.

One night, while sitting alone in his empty office, Fred cried out to God: **"I've ruined everything. Can You still use me?"** In that moment, Fred felt a quiet assurance: **"Your story isn't over."**

He began to rebuild, not just his finances, but his faith. He apologized to his family, sought wise counsel, and started a new business with humility and prayer. Today, Fred shares his story to encourage others, reminding them that failure is not final when God is involved.

Here are some lessons you can learn from regret:

- **Regret is a Teacher, Not a Master** - Learn from your mistakes, but don't let them define you.

- **God's Grace is Bigger than Your Failure** - His forgiveness is complete, and His love is unconditional.

- **You Are Not Alone** - Others have walked through regret and found redemption. You, too, can.

- **Your Mistakes Don't Disqualify You** - God can use even your failures for His glory.

- **Healing Takes Time** - Be patient with yourself as you rebuild trust and confidence.

Past mistakes can be personal, professional, or even spiritual. Recovering from mistakes isn't about erasing the past; it's about rewriting your response to it.

Biblical points of view on recovering from past mistakes:

"For all have sinned, and come short of the glory of God." - Romans 3:23 (KJV)

"Repent ye therefore, and be converted, that your sins may be blotted out..." - Acts 3:19 (KJV)

"There is therefore now no condemnation to them which are in Christ Jesus..." - Romans 8:1 (KJV)

How do you recover from past mistakes?

- **Own It Without Over-identifying:** Admit the mistake clearly and humbly, but don't let it become your identity. You made a mistake; you are not a mistake.

- **Reflect, Don't Ruminate:** Ask: What led to this? What can I learn? Reflection leads to growth. Rumination leads to shame. Choose the path that builds, not breaks.

- **Make Amends Where Possible:** If your mistake affected others, take responsibility and offer a sincere apology. Repairing trust takes time, but humility opens the door.

- **Create a New Pattern:** Mistakes often reveal weak spots in habits, boundaries, or decision-making. Use the insight to build new rhythms that protect your future.

- **Move Forward with Grace:** Don't wait until you "feel worthy" again. Grace is the bridge between regret and restoration. Walk it boldly.

Regret doesn't have to be the end of your story. It can be the beginning of something new. God's grace is greater than your mistakes, and His love is deeper than your shame.

Step out of the room called regret and into the freedom of forgiveness. Let God rebuild what's been broken and use your story to bring hope to others.

Your past doesn't define you; God does.

As you reflect on these words, find a quiet, comfortable space and lift these prayers from your heart. Know that you are not alone; many men across the world are kneeling with you as you break free from the holds of past mistakes.

PRAYER POINTS – MEN HAUNTED BY PAST MISTAKES

1. Lord, I bring my mistakes to You - the ones I've spoken of and the ones I've buried. Cleanse me from the guilt that still lingers. You said if I confess my sins, You are faithful to forgive and cleanse me. I believe You are doing that for me now (1 John 1:9).

2. Father, heal me from the shame that has kept me bound. I've worn it like a shadow, but today, I lift my eyes to believe again. Your Word says whoever believes in You shall not be ashamed. Let that truth be louder than my past (Romans 10:11).

3. Lord, I need wisdom, not just to regret what I've done, but to live differently from here. Teach me to make better choices. You promised to give wisdom freely to those who ask, and so I ask, believing You will guide me (James 1:5).

4. Father, restore what I lost - years, trust, peace, even identity. You are the God who restores what the locusts have eaten. Rebuild what was broken. Revive what died in me. Redeem my story for Your glory (Joel 2:25).

5. Lord, give me the courage to face the consequences of my actions with humility. I don't want to run, I want to grow. Strengthen me to walk through this process knowing that You are with me wherever I go (Joshua 1:9).

6. Father, break the chains of regret that still hold me hostage. I am tired of replaying the past. You said I'm no longer bound, that Christ has made me free. Help me to walk boldly in that freedom (Galatians 5:1).

7. Lord, remind me that You can still bring good from what I got wrong. Even my deepest failures are not beyond Your reach. Work all things, even this, for good, because I love You and I'm called by Your purpose (Romans 8:28).

8. Father, breathe fresh hope into me. When it feels like I've ruined too much, whisper again that my story isn't over. You have plans for me - plans of peace, not evil, to give me a future and a hope (Jeremiah 29:11).

9. Lord, help me forgive myself. I know You've forgiven me, but I still struggle to let go. Drown every voice of condemnation with the truth that there is now no condemnation for those who are in Christ Jesus (Romans 8:1).

10. Father, use this pain for a purpose. Let my mistakes become a message of Your mercy. Show me how to help others find healing through what I've walked through. Establish me, strengthen me, and settle me by Your grace (1 Peter 5:10).

CHAPTER 21

THE MAN WHO LISTENS

A Letter to Men Learning Emotional Intelligence

Dear Brother,

Listening is more than hearing words; it's understanding hearts. It's the ability to pause, to empathize, and to respond with wisdom instead of reaction.

But let's be honest: listening doesn't come naturally to many of us. We're often quick to fix, to defend, or to dismiss. Emotional intelligence - the art of understanding and managing emotions in ourselves and others - is a skill that requires humility, patience, and practice.

The man who listens is the man who leads with love. He builds bridges instead of walls, creates safe spaces for others to share their burdens, and reflects the heart of God, who listens to us in our deepest need.

Let me share with you the story of Peter – **"The Father Who Learned to Listen"**

Peter was a hardworking father who loved his family deeply. But his teenage son, Zach, often felt unheard. Whenever Zach tried to share his struggles, Peter would interrupt with advice or dismiss his feelings as "just a phase."

One day, Zach broke down in tears and said, **"Dad, you never listen to me. You just tell me what to do."**

Peter was stunned. He realized that his good intentions, trying to fix things, had made Zach feel invisible. That night, Peter prayed for wisdom and asked God to help him become a better listener.

The next time Zach opened up, Peter did something different: he stayed silent. He nodded, asked questions, and let Zach express himself fully. For the first time, Zach felt heard. Their relationship began to heal, and Peter learned that listening wasn't about having the right answers; it was about being present.

Here are some lessons from emotional intelligence:

- **Listening is an Act of Love** - When you truly listen, you show others that they matter.

- **Empathy Builds Connection** - Understanding someone's feelings creates trust and strengthens relationships.

- **Pause Before You React** - Emotional intelligence means responding thoughtfully, not impulsively.

- **Listening Requires Humility** - It's not about proving you're right; it's about understanding the other person's perspective.

- **God is the Ultimate Listener** - He hears us in our pain, our joy, and our silence. We can reflect His heart by listening well.

Developing emotional intelligence, especially the kind that helps men become better listeners, isn't just about technique; it's about transformation - not about becoming less masculine, but becoming more whole. Silence isn't weakness; it's wisdom.

Here are Biblical points of view on emotional intelligence:

"Let us search and try our ways, and turn again to the Lord." - Lamentations 3:40 (KJV)

"He that is slow to anger is better than the mighty; and he that ruleth his spirit than he that taketh a city." - Proverbs 16:32 (KJV)

"But the fruit of the Spirit is love, joy, peace, longsuffering, gentleness, goodness, faith, meekness, temperance..." - Galatians 5:22–23 (KJV)

Finally, how can you continually develop balanced emotional intelligence?

- **Cultivate Self-Awareness:**
  - Pay attention to your emotional triggers and patterns.
  - Journal your thoughts and reactions to daily events.
  - Ask: "What am I feeling?" and "Why am I feeling this?"

- **Practice Emotional Regulation**
  - Learn to pause before reacting, especially in conflict.
  - Use breathing techniques or short walks to reset.
  - Replace impulsive responses with thoughtful reflection.

- **Strengthen Empathy**
  - Listen to understand, not to fix: Instead of jumping in with advice or correction, pause and let the other person finish.
  - Many men default to problem-solving. But sometimes, people just want to be heard.
  - Ask open-ended questions like "What was that like for you?" or "How did that make you feel?"
  - Validate others' emotions, even if you don't agree with them.

- **Improve Communication Skills**
  - ○ Use "I feel..." statements instead of blame.
  - ○ Be mindful of tone, body language, and timing.
  - ○ Practice active listening: eye contact, nodding, and silence.

- **Seek Feedback and Growth**
  - ○ Ask trusted friends or mentors how you show up emotionally.
  - ○ Join men's groups or workshops focused on emotional development.
  - ○ Read books or take courses on emotional intelligence and relational health.

Listening is a skill, but it's also a posture of the heart. It's about valuing others enough to hear their stories, their struggles, and their dreams.

The man who listens is the man who loves deeply, leads wisely, and reflects the heart of God. As you grow in emotional intelligence, remember that God listens to you in every moment, and He's teaching you to do the same for others.

You're not just learning to listen; you're learning to love.

As you reflect on these words, find a quiet, comfortable space and lift these prayers from your heart. Know that you are not alone; many men across the world are kneeling with you to journey towards emotional intelligence.

PRAYER POINTS – MEN LEARNING EMOTIONAL INTELLIGENCE

1. Lord, give me wisdom to listen beyond words - to hear with understanding, not just respond with impatience. Teach me how to pause, reflect, and lean in. You said if I lack wisdom, I should ask, and You will give liberally. I ask You now, and I wait with a teachable heart (James 1:5).

2. Father, let every conversation begin with humility. Deliver me from the need to prove a point or win an argument. Help me esteem others above myself and speak with grace rather than pride (Philippians 2:3).

3. Lord, make me sensitive to the emotions of those around me. Teach me not only to speak but to feel, to rejoice when others rejoice, and to weep when they weep. Let empathy live in me (Romans 12:15).

4. Father, help me pause before I react. Train me to be slow to anger, thoughtful in my responses, and self-controlled in my emotions. You said the one who rules his spirit is greater than one who takes a city. Make me that man (Proverbs 16:32).

5. Lord, let my listening become a bridge for healing. Where trust has been broken and relationships strained, use my ears more than my mouth. Let soft answers carry Your peace and disarm offense (Proverbs 15:1).

6. Father, when I feel misunderstood, teach me to be patient. Let me stay gentle in hard conversations,

and not give in to the urge to fight for clarity over compassion. You've called me to be patient and kind to all men (2 Timothy 2:24).

7. Lord, purify my words. Let them be seasoned with salt - words that uplift, heal, and guide. Don't let my speech bring harm or confusion, but always reflect the tone of heaven (Colossians 4:6).

8. Father, create in me a heart that listens, not passively, but deeply. Teach me to be swift to hear, slow to speak, and even slower to get angry. Shape in me the posture of a wise and loving man (James 1:19).

9. Lord, help me overcome every root of pride that keeps me from truly listening. Help me recognize when I've become unteachable, defensive, or closed off. Pride goes before destruction, and I want to choose humility before I fall (Proverbs 16:18).

10. Father, help me reflect You, the God who listens when His children cry. Make me approachable, present, and tenderhearted. Let those around me know they are heard, not just spoken to, because I carry Your nature (Psalm 34:15).

CHAPTER 22

THE WOUND FROM THE HOUSE OF FRIENDS

A Letter to Men Healing from Church Hurt

Dear Brother,

There's no pain quite like the pain that comes from the house of God - the place you trusted to be a sanctuary becoming a battlefield and the ones you called brothers becoming strangers, or worse, enemies, the leaders you admired falling short, and the community you served leaving you feeling abandoned, betrayed, or even used.

Church hurt is real. It cuts deep because it strikes at the heart of your faith, your identity, and your relationships. It can leave you questioning not just people, but God Himself. *"Lord, how could this happen in Your house?"*

Let's sit and listen to the story of Marcus – **"The Men's Leader Who Walked Away"**

Marcus was a faithful church member for years. He led the men's fellowship, gave generously, and served quietly behind the scenes. But after a leadership dispute where he spoke out against financial misconduct, he was quietly pushed out - meetings stopped, phone calls went unanswered, and ministry doors closed.

Gossip spread about him in the name of *"let us pray for Bro. Marcus"*. Embarrassed, bitter, and heartbroken, Marcus stopped attending church altogether. For months, he drifted, clinging to podcasts and private worship, but he missed the joy of fellowship. It wasn't until a spiritual mentor lovingly reached out that Marcus began to process the pain.

Healing didn't come overnight. There were tears, hard conversations, and forgiveness that didn't always feel fair. Marcus later chose to return to the feet of Jesus, not the applause of men. Today, he worships again, not blindly, but boldly. His scars became wisdom. His love for the Church deepens because it is rooted in grace, not people-pleasing.

Let me share with you some lessons from church hurt:

- **God is Not the Author of Your Pain** - People may fail, but God's character remains faithful and true.

- **Healing Takes Time** - It's okay to grieve, but don't let bitterness take root.

- **Forgiveness is Freedom** - Forgiving those who hurt you doesn't excuse their actions; it releases you from their hold.

- **The Church is Still God's Plan** - Despite its flaws, the Church is the body of Christ, and He calls us to be part of it.

- **Your Pain Can Become Your Ministry** - God can use your story to bring healing to others who are hurting.

Brother, the wounds you carry are real, but they don't have to define you. God sees your pain, and He is near to the brokenhearted. Let Him heal you, restore you, and remind you that His love is greater than the failures of men.

Remember, at the judgment seat of Christ, pain and hurt alone won't be enough to absolve the choices made.

Here are Biblical points of view on church hurt:

"For it was not an enemy that reproached me; then I could have borne it… but it was thou, a man mine equal, my guide, and mine acquaintance."
- Psalm 55:12–13 (KJV)

"If it be possible, as much as lieth in you, live peaceably with all men." - Romans 12:18 (KJV)

"If thy brother shall trespass against thee, go and tell him his fault between thee and him alone…"

So, dear Brother, how do you begin to heal?

- **Acknowledge the Hurt** - Pretending you're "over it" doesn't heal it. Be honest with God, yourself, and with someone safe.

- **Separate God from Man** - God's character is not defined by human failure. His love remains untouched by what others did.

- **Forgive, but with Boundaries** - Forgiveness is required. Access isn't. Let go, but don't rush into unsafe spaces.

- **Stay Connected** - Don't let hurt isolate you from God's family. Healing may begin in solitude, but it matures in community.

- **Let God Rebuild You** - God doesn't just restore attendance; He restores trust, tenderness, and spiritual authority.

The Church is not perfect, but it is still God's plan to bring His kingdom to earth. Don't let the actions of a few rob you of the beauty of belonging to His body. Your story isn't over; it's just beginning.

You are not alone. God is with you, and He will walk with you every step of the way.

As you reflect on these words, find a quiet, comfortable space and lift these prayers from your heart. Know that you are not alone; many men across the world are kneeling with you as you heal from church hurts.

PRAYER POINTS – HEALING FROM CHURCH HURT

1. Lord, I bring You the wounds caused by those I once trusted. It wasn't an enemy who hurt me; it was someone I called brother, someone I walked with. Heal the deep places where betrayal pierced my soul. "For it was not an enemy that reproached me… but thou, a man mine equal, my guide, and mine acquaintance" (Psalm 55:12–13).

2. Help me, Father, to forgive those who hurt me, even when they never apologized and when it still stings. I choose forgiveness not because it's easy, but because You forgave me first. "Be kind one to another, tenderhearted, forgiving one another, even as God for Christ's sake hath forgiven you" (Ephesians 4:32).

3. Remind me that You are the Judge, not me. I don't have to carry vengeance or anger. You saw it all, and You will make things right. "Vengeance is mine; I will repay, saith the Lord" (Romans 12:19).

4. Guard my heart, Lord. Don't let bitterness take root. Pull out every seed of resentment before it chokes the life out of me. "Lest any root of bitterness springing up trouble you, and thereby many be defiled" (Hebrews 12:15).

5. Help me see the Church through Your eyes, even in its flaws. Don't let the failure of men blind me to the faithfulness of God. You are still building Your Church, and the gates of hell will not prevail against it (Matthew 16:18).

6. Give me discernment, Lord. Teach me who to trust, where to be vulnerable, and how to guard my heart without closing it. "Be wise as serpents, and harmless as doves" (Matthew 10:16).

7. Restore my hope, Lord. Show me that hurt doesn't have to be the end of my story. You still have good plans for my life - plans for peace and not for evil, to give me a future filled with hope (Jeremiah 29:11).

8. Soften my heart again. Teach me to love like You love freely, fully, and without fear. "Love one another; as I have loved you, that ye also love one another" (John 13:34).

9. Give me the courage to rebuild and return, not just to church attendance, but to true connection and trust. Help me not to grow weary in the process. "For in due season we shall reap, if we faint not" (Galatians 6:9).

10. Fill every broken place in me with Your peace, Lord. Where pain has lived too long, move in with healing. "He healeth the broken in heart, and bindeth up their wounds" (Psalm 147:3).

CHAPTER 23

THE SHEPHERD WITH A LIMP

A Letter to Pastors Who Minister While Wounded

Dear Brother,

You stand in the gap for others. You pray over them, counsel them, and carry their burdens to the throne of grace. You pour out your heart week after week, even when your own heart feels empty. You've been faithful to the call, but somewhere along the way, you've been wounded.

Maybe it was the betrayal of a trusted friend. Maybe it was the sting of criticism from those you've served tirelessly. Maybe it was the weight of grief, loss, or disappointment that no one sees. Whatever the source, the pain is real. And yet, you keep going - preaching, leading, and shepherding, even as you limp.

Here we go with the story of Pastor James – **"The Pastor Who Kept Preaching"**

Pastor James had been leading his church for over 15 years. He was known for his compassion, powerful sermons, and his unwavering commitment to his congregation. But behind the scenes, James was struggling.

A close friend and elder in the church had betrayed his trust, spreading false rumors that divided the congregation. Attendance dropped, finances dwindled, and James felt the weight of it all. He began to question his calling, wondering if he had failed as a leader.

But James kept preaching. He kept visiting the sick, counseling the hurting, and praying for his flock. It wasn't until a fellow pastor noticed the weariness in his eyes and asked, "Who's shepherding you?" that James realized he couldn't keep going on his own.

Through counseling, prayer, and the support of trusted friends, James began to heal. He learned that it was okay to admit his pain, to lean on others, and to let God minister to him in his brokenness. Today, James still carries the scars of that season, but they've become a testimony of God's faithfulness. He preaches with a deeper empathy, greater humility, and a renewed dependence on the God who strengthens him.

Here are some lessons from the limp:

- **Your Limp is Not Your Disqualification** - Just as Jacob wrestled with God and walked away with a limp, your wounds can become a mark of God's work in your life.

- **You Can't Pour from an Empty Cup** - Even shepherds need rest, renewal, and a safe place to heal.

- **God's Strength is Made Perfect in Weakness** - Your vulnerability doesn't diminish your ministry; it deepens it.

- **Healing is a Process** – It is okay to take time to grieve, process, and recover.

- **You Are Not Alone** - God is with you, and He has placed people around you to walk with you through the pain.

Dear Pastor, your limp is not a sign of failure; it's a sign that you've wrestled with God and survived. It's a reminder that His grace is sufficient, even when you feel insufficient.

You don't have to carry the weight of ministry alone. Let God tend to your wounds, surround you with trusted companions, and remind you that He is the Good Shepherd who restores your soul.

Your scars are not the end of your story; rather, they are the beginning of a deeper, richer testimony of God's faithfulness. Keep walking, even with a limp. God is with you every step of the way.

Here are Biblical points of view on betrayed Pastors:

"At my first answer no man stood with me, but all men forsook me: I pray God that it may not be laid to their charge." - 2 Timothy 4:16 (KJV)

"Dearly beloved, avenge not yourselves... for it is written, Vengeance is mine; I will repay, saith the Lord." - Romans 12:19 (KJV)

"But none of these things move me, neither count I my life dear unto myself, so that I might finish my course with joy..." - Acts 20:24 (KJV)

So, dear Pastor, how can you recover from church betrayals?

1. **Acknowledge the Wound without Shame:** You don't have to pretend it didn't hurt. Jesus was betrayed by His disciples. He understands. Naming the pain is the first step toward healing.

2. **Separate God's Character from People's Behavior:** The Church may have failed you, but God hasn't. Don't let the actions of a few distort the voice of the One who called you.

3. **Grieve What Was Lost:** Whether it was trust, friendships, reputation, or a ministry assignment, grieve it. David wept. Elijah withdrew. Even Jesus wept over Jerusalem. Grief is not weakness; it's worship in the language of lament.

4. **Seek Safe, Spirit-Filled Counsel:** Find a mentor, counselor, or fellow pastor who can walk with you. Healing accelerates in safe spaces where you're not "Pastor"- you're just a son of God.

5. **Forgive, Even If You Never Get an Apology:** Forgiveness is not agreement; it's release. It frees your heart from bitterness and makes room for joy again.

6. **Rest Without Guilt:** You are not your pulpit. You are not your productivity. Take time to rest, retreat, and let God minister to *you*.

7. **Rebuild Slowly and Prayerfully:** Don't rush back into ministry to prove you're okay. Let God reestablish your footing. Sometimes the next assignment is not a platform; it's a prayer closet.

8. **Let the Limp Become Your Language:** Like Jacob, your limp can become your legacy. You'll preach differently, love deeper, and lead with more grace. That's not failure; it's transformation.

As you reflect on these words, find a quiet, comfortable space and lift these prayers from your heart. Know that you are not alone; many men across the world are kneeling with you as you recover from ministry battle wounds.

PRAYER POINTS – MINISTERING WHILE WOUNDED

1. Lord, remind me that Your strength doesn't come when I'm at my best, but when I'm at my weakest. Let Your power rest on me even when I feel broken. "My grace is sufficient for thee: for my strength is made perfect in weakness" (2 Corinthians 12:9).

2. Heal me, Lord, from the wounds inflicted by those I once trusted; those who should've held my arms up, not pierced my back. You know this pain too well. "For it was not an enemy that reproached me… but thou, a man mine equal, my guide, and mine acquaintance" (Psalm 55:12–13).

3. Teach me to rest in You, not just physically but in soul and spirit. When I'm weary from pouring out, draw me back to Your embrace. "Come unto me, all ye that labour and are heavy laden, and I will give you rest" (Matthew 11:28).

4. Give me wisdom to keep leading, even when it's hard. Let me not lead from pressure but from posture, kneeling before You first. "If any of you lack wisdom, let him ask of God… and it shall be given him" (James 1:5).

5. Guard my heart, Father. Don't let bitterness become my response to betrayal. Uproot resentment before it

becomes a stronghold. "Lest any root of bitterness springing up trouble you, and thereby many be defiled" (Hebrews 12:15).

6. Help me to forgive, even when I'm bleeding. Let mercy flow before memory. Even if I never hear 'sorry,' teach me to let go. "Forgiving one another, even as God for Christ's sake hath forgiven you" (Ephesians 4:32).

7. Restore my joy, Lord. Let the ministry not feel like a burden, but a gift again. Rekindle the fire of my calling. "Restore unto me the joy of thy salvation; and uphold me with thy free spirit" (Psalm 51:12).

8. Remind me that I'm not alone in this pain. You are near to the brokenhearted, and You see every tear no one else does. "The LORD is nigh unto them that are of a broken heart" (Psalm 34:18).

9. Give me the courage to admit when I'm not okay. Help me open up to trusted voices who can pray with me and walk with me. "Confess your faults one to another… that ye may be healed" (James 5:16).

10. Strengthen me to keep going. When I feel tired of carrying others, carry me. Let me run and not be weary. Let me walk and not faint. "But they that wait upon the LORD shall renew their strength…" (Isaiah 40:31).

CHAPTER 24

STRONG FOR HER

A Letter to Husbands About Love, Honor & Covenant

Dear Brother,

Strength isn't just about muscles or power; it's about character. As husbands, we are called to be strong for our wives, not just physically, but emotionally, spiritually, and relationally. This strength isn't about dominance; it's about service. It's about loving her as Christ loves the church, honoring her as a precious gift, and keeping the covenant we made before God.

Let's see through the lens of **"Michael's turning point."**

Michael and Sarah had been married for ten years, but their relationship was struggling. Michael was a good provider, but he often felt distant and disconnected from Sarah. He thought his role as a husband was just about paying bills and fixing problems, but Sarah longed for emotional connection and spiritual leadership.

One night, after a heated argument, Sarah broke down in tears. She told Michael she felt alone in their marriage. Her words hit him hard. Michael realized he had been neglecting the most important part of his role: loving and honoring Sarah as Christ loves the church.

Michael decided to make a change. He started praying for Sarah every morning, asking God to help him be the husband she needed. He began listening to her more, asking about her dreams and fears. He also started leading their family in prayer and Bible study, something he had avoided for years.

Over time, their marriage transformed. Sarah felt loved and valued, and Michael discovered the joy of being strong for her, not just in providing, but in loving, honoring, and leading.

Here are some Scriptural points of view:

"Husbands, love your wives, even as Christ also loved the church, and gave himself for it"
- Ephesians 5:25 (KJV).

"Likewise, ye husbands, dwell with them according to knowledge, giving honor unto the wife, as unto the weaker vessel, and as being heirs together of the grace of life; that your prayers be not hindered"
- 1 Peter 3:7 (KJV).

"Husbands, love your wives, and be not bitter against them" - Colossians 3:19 (KJV).

Dear Brother, what does it mean to be strong for your wife?

- **Love Her Sacrificially** - True love puts her needs above your own. It's not about what you can get; it's about what you can give.

- **Honor Her Deeply** - Treat her with respect and kindness, valuing her as God's gift to you.

- **Lead Her Spiritually** - Be the spiritual leader of your home, guiding her and your family closer to God.

- **Protect Her Heart** - Guard her emotions and build trust through honesty and faithfulness.

- **Pray for Her Daily** - Cover her in prayer, asking God to bless, strengthen, and guide her.

Being strong for her means showing up when it's hard, listening when she's hurting, and leading with humility and grace. It means protecting her heart, providing for her needs, and praying for her daily. It's not about being perfect; rather, it's about being present.

This kind of strength doesn't come from us; it comes from God. When we rely on Him, He equips us to be the husbands that our wives need and deserve.

As you reflect on these words, find a quiet, comfortable space and lift these prayers from your heart. Know that you are not alone; many men across the world are kneeling with you to journey towards unwavering devotion, commitment and love to our wives.

PRAYER POINTS – HUSBAND'S LOVE, HONOR & COVENANT

1. Lord, help me love my wife as You love the Church - sacrificially, fully, and faithfully. Let my actions mirror Your heart. Teach me to lay down selfishness and lead with selfless devotion. "Husbands, love your wives, even as Christ also loved the church, and gave himself for it" (Ephesians 5:25).

2. Teach me to honor my wife, not only in public but in the unseen moments. Let my words, my tone, and my thoughts reflect the value You've placed on her. "Giving honour unto the wife… being heirs together of the grace of life" (1 Peter 3:7).

3. Sanctify our intimacy, Lord. Let our physical union reflect purity and covenant joy. Guard my heart and eyes from every distraction, and keep me loyal in body and desire. "Let the husband render unto the wife due benevolence…" (1 Corinthians 7:3).

4. Give me patience when things are tense. Help me choose understanding over assumption. Make me gentle and long-suffering, willing to listen deeply

and love through difficulty. "With all lowliness and meekness, with longsuffering, forbearing one another in love" (Ephesians 4:2).

5. Keep me faithful, Lord, not just in action but in thought and intention. Let my fountain be blessed, and teach me to rejoice daily in the gift of my wife. "Rejoice with the wife of thy youth" (Proverbs 5:18).

6. Help me guard my wife's heart. Let me protect not just her safety, but her emotions, dignity, and peace. Strengthen me to shield our covenant from any attack. "What therefore God hath joined together, let not man put asunder" (Matthew 19:6).

7. When tension rises, give me wisdom to de-escalate with humility. Let me lay pride aside and be the first to seek peace, even when it's hard. "Only by pride cometh contention: but with the well advised is wisdom" (Proverbs 13:10).

8. Make us one in every way - spiritually, emotionally, and mentally. Teach us to cleave to each other with a bond that only You can strengthen. "They shall be one flesh" (Genesis 2:24).

9. Help me forgive quickly and seek forgiveness humbly. Let our marriage be a safe place for grace, where love restores and mercy flows freely. "Be ye kind one to another, tenderhearted, forgiving one another..." (Ephesians 4:32).

10. Strengthen me daily, Lord. When I fall short, lift me. When I'm tired, renew me. Help me become the husband You've called me to be. "I can do all things through Christ, which strengtheneth me" (Philippians 4:13).

CHAPTER 25

NEARING HOME

A Letter to Men Preparing for the Final Season of Life

Dear Brother,

There comes a time in every man's life when the road ahead grows shorter than the road behind. It's a season of reflection, of quiet surrender, and of preparing to meet the One who gave us life. This isn't a time to fear; it's a time to embrace.

Nearing home doesn't mean you're finished; it means you're being perfected. It's a season to pass on wisdom, reconcile relationships, and deepen your walk with God. It's a time to leave behind a legacy that speaks louder than possessions - a legacy of faith, love, and forgiveness.

Let's listen to John – **"The Farmer Who Found Peace in His Final Season."**

John was a farmer who spent his life working the land and providing for his family. He was known for his hard work and quiet strength, but as the years passed, his health began to decline. At 78, John knew his time was nearing.

One evening, as he sat on his porch watching the sunset, he felt a deep stirring in his heart. He realized there were things he needed to make right before he left this world. He had grown distant from his eldest son after a bitter argument years ago, and he hadn't spoken to him since.

With trembling hands, John wrote a letter to his son. In it, he apologized for his pride and asked for forgiveness. He shared memories of their time on the farm and expressed his love for him. A week later, his son came to visit, and they reconciled with tears and hugs.

John spent his final months writing letters to each of his children and grandchildren, sharing his faith, love, and his hopes for their future. He passed away peacefully, surrounded by family, leaving behind a legacy of reconciliation and grace.

Here are some lessons from nearing home:

- **Make Peace with Your Past** - Let go of regrets and embrace God's forgiveness.

- **Reconcile Relationships** - Seek forgiveness and offer grace to those you've hurt or been hurt by.

- **Pass on Wisdom** - Share your faith, values, and lessons with the next generation.

- **Deepen Your Walk with God** - Spend time in prayer, worship, and reflection as you prepare to meet Him.

- **Live with Eternity in View** - Remember that this life is temporary, but eternity is forever.

Biblical points of view on men nearing home call:

"And as it is appointed unto men once to die, but after this the judgment." - Hebrews 9:27 (KJV)

"Wherefore the rather, brethren, give diligence to make your calling and election sure…" - 2 Peter 1:10 (KJV)

"Henceforth there is laid up for me a crown of righteousness… unto all them also that love his appearing." - 2 Timothy 4:8 (KJV)

Dear Brother, these are ways to prepare for the final season of life while enjoying the moment:

- **Reflect on Your Journey**

  ○ Take time to look back with honesty and gratitude.

  ○ Write down key lessons, defining moments, and people who shaped you.

  ○ Let your story become a legacy, not just a memory.

- **Reconcile Relationships**
    - Reach out to those you've hurt or who've hurt you.
    - Offer forgiveness, even if you never get an apology.
    - Healing doesn't require perfection; it requires humility.

- **Clarify Your Spiritual Standing**
    - Spend time in prayer, Scripture, and worship.
    - Ask yourself: "Am I at peace with God?"
    - If not, this is the season to surrender fully and walk closely.

- **Pass On Wisdom**
    - Write letters to your children, grandchildren, or mentees.
    - Share your faith, your failures, and your hopes for their future.
    - Your words may outlive you and guide them when you're gone.

- **Organize Your Affairs**
    - Prepare your will, legacy documents, and final wishes.

- ○ Make sure your loved ones know your desires — spiritually and practically.

- ○ This isn't morbid; it's merciful.

- **Live with Eternity in View**

    - ○ Let go of the need to control outcomes.

    - ○ Embrace simplicity, joy, and presence.

    - ○ Eternity isn't far; it's near, and it's beautiful.

- **Finish Well**

    - ○ You don't have to be perfect; you just have to be faithful.

    - ○ Let your final season be marked by grace, generosity, and peace.

    - ○ The goal isn't to leave a monument; it's to leave a message.

Nearing home is not the end; it's the beginning of eternity. It's a season to reflect, reconcile, and rejoice in the promise of eternal life. You may feel weak, but God's strength is made perfect in your weakness. You may feel uncertain, but His peace surpasses all understanding.

As you prepare to meet your Maker, remember that you are His beloved son. He has walked with you through every season of life, and He will carry you into eternity with grace and love.

Finish well, brother. Leave behind a legacy of faith, forgiveness, and hope. And when the time comes to cross over, know that you are going home, not as a stranger, but as a son.

As you reflect on these words, find a quiet, comfortable space and lift these prayers from your heart. Know that you are not alone; many men across the world are kneeling with you to make everyday count in eternity.

PRAYER POINTS – MEN PREPARING FOR FINAL SEASON OF LIFE

1. Lord, grant me peace as I prepare to meet You. Settle my mind and quiet my soul with the assurance of eternity. I fix my thoughts on You, trusting that You will keep me in perfect peace. "Thou wilt keep him in perfect peace, whose mind is stayed on thee: because he trusteth in thee" (Isaiah 26:3).

2. Father, help me reflect on my life with humility and gratitude. Let me see my journey through the lens of Your mercy, not just my achievements. "Examine me, O LORD, and prove me; try my reins and my heart" (Psalm 26:2).

3. Give me the courage to seek forgiveness and make peace where needed. Let kindness mark my final season, and tenderheartedness define my legacy. "Forgiving one another, even as God for Christ's sake hath forgiven you" (Ephesians 4:32).

4. Guide me, Lord, as I pass on my faith and wisdom. Let the steps of my life speak to my children and those who come after me. "The just man walketh in his integrity: his children are blessed after him" (Proverbs 20:7).

5. Thank You for the promise of eternal life. When earthly things fade, let Your eternal Word anchor my hope. "And this is the promise that he hath promised us, even eternal life" (1 John 2:25).

6. Strengthen me, Father. As my body grows weak, let my spirit remain strong in You. Remind me that Your grace is enough for every day ahead. "My grace is sufficient for thee: for my strength is made perfect in weakness" (2 Corinthians 12:9).

7. Help me live each remaining day with thanksgiving. I thank You not only for the blessings but also for the lessons, trusting that You've been with me through them all. "In everything give thanks: for this is the will of God in Christ Jesus concerning you" (1 Thessalonians 5:18).

8. Teach me to rest in Your timing. Even when I don't understand, I surrender to Your divine calendar and trust in Your perfect will. "To everything there is a season, and a time to every purpose under the heaven" (Ecclesiastes 3:1).

9. Fill my heart with hope, Lord. As I prepare for eternity, remind me that I have a heavenly home not made with hands, where You await me. "We have a building of God… eternal in the heavens" (2 Corinthians 5:1).

10. Let my life and death glorify You. Whether in my remaining days or my final breath, may I testify that I belong to the Lord. "For whether we live… or die, we are the Lord's" (Romans 14:8).